147 Fun Things To Do In ATLANTA

written by
KAREN FOULK

INTO FUN, COMPANY
PUBLICATIONS
A Division of Into Fun, Inc.
Sugar Land, Texas

147 Fun Things To Do In Atlanta
by Karen Foulk

Cover and Map illustrations by Delton Gerdes
Book Layout by Karen Foulk
with assistance from Brockton Publishing Company

Copyright © 2001 Karen Foulk

All rights reserved. No part of this book may be reproduced or transmitted in any form or by any means, electronic, mechanical, photocopying, recording or otherwise, without prior written permission from the publisher.
Printed in Canada

Library of Congress Catalog Card Number:
2001 131338

ISBN 0-9652464-8-5

INTO FUN, INC.
P.O. Box 2494, Sugar Land, Texas 77487-2494
Phone: 281-980-9745 Fax: 281-494-9745

Find us on the internet:
www.intofun.com

This book contains descriptions including operating times and admission costs of many of the fun and interesting places in the Atlanta area. Although a great deal of effort has gone into making this book as up-to-date and accurate as possible, changes constantly occur. Therefore, before visiting a destination, please call to confirm the information provided herein. Neither Into Fun, Co. Publications, a division of Into Fun, Inc., the owner, nor the author warrant the accuracy of the information in this book which includes but is not limited to price changes, addresses, names, hours of operation, management or conditions of the attraction described.

Dedication

With all my love,

*To my husband, Don,
who thinks I'm having too much fun.*

Michael & Amber

Rachel & John

David

Rebecca

Acknowledgments

Again in appreciation for their contributions,
to the many dear friends, family members,
and associates who make this book possible.

To my husband and children,
for putting up with a busy mom.

To Jerrie Hurd my loving sister.

To Merrill Littlewood, my accountant.
He's the best.

To Michael Foulk, for being N2Fun's webmaster.

To Ken Barrow, for his legal help and advice.

To Annette Hruska, for designing the N2Fun car.

To Sharon Cooper, always a friend.

To John Kessler, the dining critic for the Atlanta
Journal–Constitution. He contributed our
restaurant recommendations.

I know people are having fun when I see them packing around my book and it's dog-eared. I'm tempted to give them mine, but it's always dog-eared too. Atlanta is that great.

Ok, I realize that my fun may not be your fun, but in Atlanta everyone finds fun.

If you enjoy history, Atlanta talks. Visiting the many museums and historic sites is a treat. In fact, you can rent a historian for the day and take him or her to all the Civil War sites. That way, you don't miss the goodstuff.

Atlanta's perfect for those who love stock car racing, hot air ballooning, hiking, kayaking, or any other sport. How about hiking the Appalachian Trail? Starting in Atlanta, the Appalacian Trail can be a day trip or an any length adventure. You decide.

If you're a high-brow, you already know about Atlanta's opera, ballet, and live theater. But do you know about the High Museum of Art?

Go see the panda bears at the zoo, the Egyptian ballroom above the Fox Theatre, and the storytellers at the Wren's Nest. Taste some of the exotic soft drinks from far-off countries like Mozambique at the World of Coca-Cola. Believe me, they give the "Real Thing" no competition.

If the "hot" sign is on at Krispy Kreme Donuts, stop in, everyone else does.

Watch canine frisbee competitions at the Dogwood Festival. Eat a catered picnic under shady oaks before watching Shakespeare. Begin the 4th of July celebration with the Peachtree Road Race. All that and much more is Atlanta.

So turn down the corners of all the pages you like and go! Get with Atlanta.

Karen Foulk

Table of Contents

What's Fun In Atlanta?...................... 9

The Great Outdoors 43

Atlanta's Museums and History.............. 71

Theaters and The Arts 91

Amusement Parks, Attractions, Tours,
        Extreme Sports and More......... 107

Eating Out In Atlanta? 127

Where to Stay? 151

Unique Places to Shop.................... 161

Annual Events 171

Index................................... 184

Locations:

1. Atlanta Cyclorama
2. Vortex Restaurant
3. MARTA
4. The Varsity
5. CNN Center
6. Atlanta History Center
7. Turner Field
8. Peachtree Street
9. Fernbank Museum
10. AtlanTIX
11. High Museum of Art
12. Martin Luther King, Jr. National Historic Site
13. Stone Mountain
14. Margaret Mitchell's House
15. Michael C. Carlos Museum
16. Atlanta Botanical Garden
17. Zoo Atlanta
18. Swan House
19. Chattahoochee River
20. Piedmont Park
21. Centennial Olympic Park
22. Underground Atlanta
23. Governor's Mansion
24. Coca-Cola Atlanta
25. Krispy Kreme Donuts
26. Fox Theatre
27. Georgia Dome
28. Wren's Nest
29. Westin Peachtree Plaza Hotel
30. State Capitol Building
31. Oakland Cemetery

Chapter 1
WHAT'S FUN IN ATLANTA?

Atlanta Cyclorama: Only a Few Left in the World 11
Best Burgers in Town at the
    Funky **Vortex Restaurant** 12
Breeze through Atlanta on **MARTA** 13
Chili Dogs, Onion Rings, and Frosted Orange Drinks
    at **The Varsity,** the World's Largest Drive-in .. 14
CNN Center and Studio Tour 15
Discover Old Atlanta at the
    Atlanta History Center 16
Dollar Tickets to Baseball Games at **Turner Field** . 17
Drive **Peachtree Street** 18
Friday Night Dinner and IMAX Show at the
    Fernbank Museum of Natural History 19
Half-Price Tickets at the **AtlanTIX** 20
High Museum of Art is a Work of Art 21
"I Have a Dream" and the **Martin Luther King, Jr.
    National Historic Site** 22
Lasershow and a Tram Ride to the Top of
    Georgia's **Stone Mountain** 23
Margaret Mitchell's House and
    Gone With the Wind Memorabilia 24
Mummies at the **Michael C. Carlos Museum** 25
New Children's Garden at the
    Atlanta Botanical Garden 26
Pandas at the **Zoo Atlanta** 27

WHAT'S FUN IN ATLANTA?
continued

Photo Opportunities at the **Swan House** 28
Rafting the **Chattahoochee River** 29
Rollerblade **Piedmont Park** 30
Run through the Fountains at
    Centennial Olympic Park 31
Shop **Underground Atlanta** 32
State Trooper Opens the Gate at the
    Georgia **Governor's Mansion** 33
Taste the World of **Coca-Cola Atlanta** 34
The "Hot" Sign at **Krispy Kreme Donuts** 35
Tour the **Fox Theatre** 36
Tour the **Georgia Dome** 37
Uncle Remus Stories at **Wren's Nest** 38
View Atlanta atop the **Westin**
    Peachtree Plaza Hotel 39
Visit the Newly Restored **State Capitol Building** .. 40
Who's Who at the **Oakland Cemetery** 41

What's Fun In Atlanta?

ATLANTA CYCLORAMA: ONLY A FEW LEFT IN THE WORLD

800 Cherokee Avenue S.E.
Atlanta 30315
404-624-1071
www.bcaatlanta.org

Only in Atlanta, see it to believe it

What's a Cyclorama? It's like a 1920s version of an IMAX show. Rather than a high-tech film, watch a 3-D diorama in the round. Only your seat moves.

The massive painting (in the diorama) depicts the Battle of Atlanta. And a larger-than-life General Sherman in his glory. After all, he commissioned the work.

It was the Atlanta Campaign that brought about President Lincoln's re-election and eventually the South's defeat. Not recommended for small children. Shows start every half hour. Afterwards, browse through the museum's fine collection of Civil War artifacts.

Hours

(Open until 5:30 pm in the summer)

Daily . . . . 9:20 – 4:30 pm

Cost

Adults $5
Children 6-12 . . . . $3
Seniors 60+ $4

Directions

Take I-20 E to exit Boulevard, turn right (south) onto Boulevard, turn right again onto Berne St. and follow into Grant Park. MARTA: Bus #31 from Five Points Station.

What's Fun In Atlanta?

BEST BURGERS IN TOWN AT THE FUNKY VORTEX RESTAURANT

438 Moreland Avenue
Atlanta 30307
404-688-1828

Tavern with an attitude

This perpetual winner of Atlanta's best burger awards is a tavern with attitude. Even the menu itself barks snarky orders at customers, with a long list of do's and don'ts, and an admonition to would-be whiners.

We admit to preferring the Midtown branch with its grungy bar atmosphere to the more sanitized offshoot in Little Five Points, which has a fern-bar look behind its groovy skull's-head entrance. The burgers and other sandwiches arrive in what seems like seconds flat and are always fat, juicy, and cooked to order.

There are any number of variations on the them. We like the Jamaican jerk burger, with its wash of spicy sauce, or the vegetarian blackbean burger. Ask for separate checks only at your peril.

Hours

Daily .... 11 am – 2 am

Cost

An Original Hamburger $5.75

Directions

Take Ponce de Leon Ave. 2 miles to Moreland Ave. Go right 2 blks. The restaurant is on the right.

What's Fun In Atlanta?

BREEZE THROUGH ATLANTA ON MARTA

Metropolitan Atlanta Rapid Transit Authority
2424 Piedmont Road
Atlanta 30324
404-848-4711

MARTA Atlanta

Remember you're looking for fun.

SAVE YOURSELF the hassles of rush hour traffic and parking. Atlanta's light rail system makes it easy.

CHEAP. Rides cost $1.75; transfers are free. (Exact change required.) Trains come every 8 – 10 minutes, depending on the time of day.

RUNS north and south, east and west. Two new station lines just added, the North Springs and the Sandy Springs.

RIDE STORES carry discount and unlimited ride tickets. Find them at Five Points, Lindbergh, and Airport stations. Maps and schedules available too.

STATIONS have token machines for single rides. Parking at MARTA station lots is free, located mostly in the suburbs.

BUS SERVICE covers 150 routes throughout Atlanta.

Hours

Mon. – Fri. . . . . 6 am – 11pm
Sat. – Sun (most holidays) . . . . . 8 am – 10 pm

Cost

One ride $1.75

Directions

Five Points station is located downtown at Peachtree and Alabama Sts.

What's Fun In Atlanta?

CHILI DOGS, ONION RINGS, AND FROSTED ORANGE DRINKS AT THE VARSITY, THE WORLD'S LARGEST DRIVE-IN

61 North Avenue N.E.
Atlanta 30308
404-881-1706

Blast from the past

This massive chrome-fronted fast food joint is a blast from the past that serves thousands daily. Part of the fun is ordering: As you go through the line and place your order, the attendant calls out the order in the Varsity's special language. A hot dog with ketchup only is a "red dog" and, as every kid in Atlanta knows, a plain hot dog is a "nekkid dog." The onion rings and fries are incredibly greasy and good, and the orange drink is a specialty.

If you don't want to eat in one of the massive dining areas, park your car and an attendant will bring a window tray in time-honored fashion.

Hours

Sun. – Thurs. . . . . 9 am – 11:30 pm
Fri. and Sat. . . . . 9 am – 12:30 pm

Cost

Chili dog $1.44
Onion Rings $1.20
Frosted Orange Drink $1.40

Directions

On North Ave. at Spring St. From downtown on Peachtree St., turn left on North Ave. The drive-in is two blocks down on the right.

What's Fun In Atlanta?

CNN CENTER AND STUDIO TOUR

One CNN Center
Atlanta 30303
404-827-2300
www.cnn.com/studiotour

CNN shows you the world, now go see CNN

A 45-minute, behind-the-scenes tour that takes you to news in the making. Begin by stepping onto the world's longest escalator; it tops out 8 stories later. You'll find this tour a high point in more ways than one.

A more in-depth tour is available for $25, but it requires reservations made a day ahead.

The giant CNN complex encompasses Ted Turner's offices, his retail shops, a mega food court, and the Omni Hotel.

Watch as the public opinion show TalkBack Live takes place out on the main floor. For free audience tickets call 800-410-CNN.

Hours

(Tours begin every 20 minutes)

Daily .... 9 am – 6 pm

Cost

(Children under 6 years of age not permitted)

Adults $8
Children 6 – 12 .... $5
Seniors 65+ $6

Directions

From Peachtree St. go east on Marietta St. (or east on International Blvd. and then right on Marietta). MARTA: Onmi/Dome/WCC Station.

What's Fun In Atlanta?

DISCOVER OLD ATLANTA AT THE ATLANTA HISTORY CENTER

130 West Paces Ferry Road, Atlanta 30325
404-814-4000 www.atlhist.org

Wandering through the museum is fun

Atlanta's story—the Battle of Atlanta—that led to the South's defeat, Martin Luther King, Jr.'s Civil Rights Movement, and Margaret Mitchell's highly acclaimed novel *Gone With The Wind*—it's all here. (No, Tara's not here in Atlanta.)

For an extra dollar, tour the old Swan House. Built in 1928, it's considered a residential masterpiece. Let your guide point out the swan motifs in the decor.

A step into Atlanta's past needs to include lunch at the Swan Coach House. Old-fashioned southern favorites include cheese straws, chicken salad, and mint juleps—always hot with the ladies.

Walk the trail that overlooks the Swan House's lush landscape gardens The gardens and house make up the most photographed site in town—so bring the camera.

Hours
Mon. – Sat.	10 am – 5:30 pm
Sunday	Noon – 5:30 pm

Cost (Museum)
(Add $1 for the Swan House tour; begins every half hour)

Adults	$10
Students 18+/ Seniors 65+	$8
Children 6 – 17	$4

Directions

In Buckhead, 2.6 miles east of I-75 and 2 blks. west of Peachtree St.. MARTA Lenox station: From there take bus #23 to Peachtree St./West Paces Ferry Rd. Walk 2 blocks west.

What's Fun In Atlanta?

DOLLAR TICKETS TO BASEBALL GAMES AT TURNER FIELD

755 Hank Aaron Drive S.W., Atlanta 30315
404-522-7630 Box Office
404-614-2311 Tours
www.atlantabraves.com

Baseball's fun at Turner Field

Baseball tickets for everyone. Get baseball tickets for as little as $1 (for skyline seats) at Turner Field. Tickets go on sale 3 hours before the game starts.

Or buy your regular-priced tickets online or at Ticketmaster, 404-817-8700, and at the box office.

Parking is limited and pricey, $7–$10. MARTA's free shuttle rides from Five Points station simplify getting there. Buses leave starting 90 minutes before a game.

Baseball memorabilia makes the **Braves Museum and Hall of Fame** the place for baseball fans. You find things like Hank Aaron's 715th home run ball and the 1995 World Series trophy. The museum opens 3 hours before a game and 1 hour after. Off season, the museum is open Mon. - Sat. 10 am – 2 pm.

Get a behind-the-scenes tour of the stadium. Offered daily, except on game days.

Hours (Box Office)
Mon. – Fri. . . . . 8:30 am – 6 pm
Saturdays . . . . 9 am – 5 pm
Sundays . . . . 1 pm – 5 pm

Cost
Regular tickets prices . . . . $5 - $35
Tours . . . . Adults $7; Children 13 & Under $4

Directions
From I-75/85, exit Fulton St./Stadium. From I-20W, exit Capitol Ave. MARTA: Five Points Station.

 *What's Fun In Atlanta?*

DRIVE PEACHTREE STREET

Scenic drive through downtown Atlanta

Traveling south of Buckhead just as Peachtree Street swings left past the Episcopal Cathedral of St. Philip, catch one of the finest views of downtown Atlanta.

What better way to show off Atlanta. You'll pass incredible sites. There's Lenox Square, the High Museum of Art, Margaret Mitchell's House, and the old historic Fox Theatre.

Atlanta's main artery—it's hard to imagine this was once an Indian trail.

What's Fun In Atlanta?

FRIDAY NIGHT DINNER AND IMAX SHOW AT THE FERNBANK MUSEUM OF NATURAL HISTORY

767 Clifton Road N.E.
Atlanta 30307
404-378-0127
www.fernbank.edu

Martinis & IMAX

Friday nights in Atlanta? Spend them at the Fernbank Museum of Natural History. Here's how to relax and have fun.

Along with your choice of an IMAX feature comes a feast—pasta, salad, chicken, steak, and seafood dishes. The evening includes live music, the museum's outstanding exhibits, and planetarium features. Call for more details.

Dress as you like; activities start at 6:30 pm. The IMAX shows begin at 7 pm, 8 pm, 9 pm, and 10 pm.

Hours

(Museum)

Monday – Saturday . . . . 10 am – 5 pm
Sunday . . . . Noon – 5 pm

Cost

(Prices vary with combination of activities)

Directions

From downtown, take Peachtree St. to Ponce de Leon Ave. Go right for 3.3 miles. Turn left on Clifton Rd. MARTA: Bus #2 from North Avenue station.

What's Fun In Atlanta?

HALF-PRICE TICKETS AT THE ATLANTIX

Atlanta Convention and Visitors Center
Underground Atlanta
65 Upper Alabama Street
Atlanta 30303
770-772-5572
www.atlantatheatres.com

First to AtlanTIX, then to the theater

If you love the theater, the AtlanTIX is an important stop. It offers 1/2-priced tickets for many of Atlanta's popular theaters.

Tickets must be purchased for that day's performances. Call for a list of participating theaters and a performance schedule.

Half-priced tickets include attractions like the Center for Puppetry Arts, the Atlanta History Center, and Zoo Atlanta. Other attractions' tickets will be available in the future.

Hours

Tuesday	11 am – 3 pm
Wed. – Sat.	11 am – 6 pm
Sunday	Noon – 3 pm

Cost

Half-price of regular tickets

Directions

On Alabama St. at Pryor St. From Peachtree St., turn southeast on Alabama St. The visitor center is one block on the left. MARTA: Five Points station.

What's Fun In Atlanta?

HIGH MUSEUM OF ART IS A WORK OF ART

1280 Peachtree Street, Atlanta 30309
404-733-4444 www.high.org

Premiere art museum

The High Museum of Art's striking white building makes its own artistic impression. Known as "one of the ten best works of American architecture of the 1980s." See why.

Holds collections significant to 19th and 20th century American art, folk art, decorative art, and English ceramics. Also hosts major traveling exhibits worth seeing. You enjoy every minute you're there.

The museum's free gallery tours take place daily. If you come on Thursdays, admission is free, 1 pm to 5 pm. Visit the nifty gift shop. The small cafe serves sandwiches and pastries. The parking garage sits behind the museum on Lombardy Way, between 15th and 16th Streets.

The museum's annex, **the High Museum of Folk Art and Photography Galleries** is downtown in the Georgia-Pacific Building at 30 John Wesley Dobbs Avenue.

Hours
Tues. - Sat.	10 am - 5 pm
4th Friday of each month	10 am - 9 pm
Sunday	Noon - 5 pm

Cost
Adults	$6
College Student/Seniors 65+	$4
Children	$2

Directions

At the corner of Peachtree and 16th Sts. in Midtown. MARTA: Arts Center.

What's Fun In Atlanta?

"I HAVE A DREAM" AND THE MARTIN LUTHER KING, JR. NATIONAL HISTORIC SITE

450 Auburn Avenue N.E.
Atlanta 30315   404-331-6922
www.nps.gov/malu

You've heard his speech, now visit the place

Visit the national historic site for America's most revered Civil Rights leader, Dr. Martin Luther King, Jr. Understand more than you ever did before about this great man and what he wanted to accomplish.

Sign up at the King Center for the Birth Home Tour. See where he lived until he was 12 years old. See the church where he preached and where he's buried.

It was at this church—The Ebenezer Church—that he planned his Civil Rights strategies. Listen to gospel music performed the 1st Saturday of the month, free. You'll find this an exciting thing to do.

Hours
(Closed Thanksgiving, Christmas, and New Year's Day)

Visitor Center
Daily (summer until 6 pm) ...... 9 am - 5 pm

Birth Home Tours
(Summer, every 1/2 hour; Winter, every 1 hour)
Daily .... 10 am - 5:30 pm

Cost
Free

Directions
From I-75/85, exit Freedom Pkwy./Carter Center. Right on Boulevard. Follow signs. MARTA: King Memorial station. Walk 8 blks. Or bus #3, Five Points station.

What's Fun In Atlanta?

LASERSHOW AND A TRAM RIDE TO THE TOP OF GEORGIA'S STONE MOUNTAIN

Highway 78
Stone Mountain 30086, 770-498-5600
www.stonemountainpark.org

See downtown Atlanta from on high

Often claimed as Georgia's most popular attraction, Stone Mountain—the world's largest mass of exposed granite is over 800 feet high. You have to see it to understand. Hike the 1.3-mile trail to the top for a breath-taking view. Or take the tram, built for the 1996 Olympic Games. The view is amazing.

On Saturday nights (March through October), the mountain's north face lights up with a 45-minute laser show. Impressive. Bring the whole family and a blanket to sit on. A must-do.

The list of fun things to do here is endless. Stone Mountain's 3200-acre park includes hiking, fishing, jogging, paddle boating, biking, golfing, tennis, and camping to name a few. Amusement-type rides: water slides, steam train, paddle wheeler, and more.

Hours

(Closed Christmas Day)
(Attraction hours varies; mostly daily 10 am - 5 pm)
Park (Daily) . . . . 6 am – midnight

Cost

(Admission to attractions varies)
Parking permits . . . . $7 or $30/year

Directions

Take Ponce de Leon Dr. going east to I-285. Take I-285 north to Stone Mountain Parkway, Highway 78.

What's Fun In Atlanta?

MARGARET MITCHELL'S HOUSE AND GONE WITH THE WIND MEMORABILIA

990 Peachtree Street
Atlanta 30309
404-249-7015
www.gwtw.org

You've seen the movie, now tour her home

Gone With The Wind still sells over 250,000 copies a year—a bestseller by any means. If you account for inflation, the movie is the world's top grossing film.

Tour the author's home. See where she wrote the novel, covering it with a towel to keep it a secret.

An Atlanta shrine—Scarlett's portrait (from the movie)—now hangs in the museum. Look closely, see where Rhett threw his drink. The painting still bears the liquor stains.

The museum holds the largest collection of *Gone With The Wind* memorabilia anywhere. The gift shop sells the movie video in many languages.

Hours

(Public tours every 1/2 hour)

Daily . . . . 9:30 am - 5 pm

Cost

Adults $10
Students/Seniors 65 + ... $8
Children 6 - 17 . . . . $5

Directions

In Midtown, at the corner of Peachtree and 10th Strs. (three 3 blocks east of I-75/85). Adjacent to the MARTA's Midtown station.

What's Fun In Atlanta?

MUMMIES AT THE MICHAEL C. CARLOS MUSEUM

Emory University Campus
571 S. Kilgo Street , Atlanta 30322
404-727-4282 General
404-727-0519 Tour schedule
www.cc.emory.edu

Remarkable Egyptology collection

Museum with dignitaries. This museum's latest acquisition includes nine mummies believed to be of ancient Egyptian royalty. In fact, the collection may include the mummy of Ramses I.

This astounding collection sat neglected for years in a Canadian museum's basement, until it was finally discovered.

The Emory Univeristy museum is one of the finest centers for Egyptian studies. It houses over 15,000 objects that span nearly 9000 years.

Free docent-lead tours on Saturday and Sunday at 2 pm. A must-do.

Hours

Mon. - Sat. . . . . 10 am - 5 pm
Sunday . . . . Noon - 5 pm

Cost

Suggested donation $5/person

Directions

On the main Quadrangle of Emory University near the Oxford Rd. gate at N. Decatur Rd. MARTA: Bus #36 (N. Decatur) from Arts Center station or Bus #6 (Emory) from Candler Park to the Oxford Rd. gate.

What's Fun In Atlanta?

NEW CHILDREN'S GARDEN AT THE ATLANTA BOTANICAL GARDEN

1345 Piedmont Avenue N.E.
Atlanta 30309
404-876-5859
www.atlantabotanicalgarden.org

Atlanta's growing adventures

Impress your kids with poisonous dart frogs, the insect-eating carnivorous plant bogs, and pebble-looking "Living Stones"(desert plants). And that's only a beginning of what you'll find fascinating.

The new children's garden—The Children's Healthcare of Atlanta Children's Garden—lets your child enjoy nature. Everything is hands-on. In the summer, kids love cooling off under the (giant) Sunflower Fountain. Come dressed to play.

Browse through their award-winning gift shop. Lunch at the Lanier Terrace Restaurant that over looks the rose garden. Roses bloom April through October.

Hours

Tues. - Sun. *(Oct. - Feb. until 6pm)* .... 9 am - 7 pm

Cost

(Free on Thursday from 3 pm until closing)

Adults $7
College Students/Children $4
Seniors $5

Directions

Piedmont Ave., between. Monroe Dr. and 14th St. MARTA Mon. - Sat. Bus #36 (N. Decatur) from Arts Center station. Sunday Bus #31 from Five Points or Lindbergh station.

What's Fun In Atlanta?

PANDAS AT THE ZOO ATLANTA

800 Cherokee Avenue S.E.
Atlanta 30315
404-624-5600
www.zooatlanta.org

Atlanta's Zoo's big on fun

Atlanta's biggest attraction—the giant pandas—is on loan from Beijing, China. One of only three zoos to have pandas. Visit them in their new $17 million habitat. Purchase "timed" tickets at the front gate to see them.

This is an old zoo, built in 1889. But it marches to the 21st century.

What's fun? Watching the animals eat, at posted feeding times. The behind-the-scenes tours and the night walks take you where zoo-goers never go.

You'll find plenty of concessions including a McDonalds. Visitors can remain inside the zoo 1 hour after closing. Open until 5:30 pm in the summer. Parking free.

Hours

(Closed Thanksgiving, Christmas, and New Year's Day)
Daily .... 9:30 am - 4:30 pm

Cost

Adults $15
Children 3 - 11 .... $10
Seniors $11

Directions

From I-20 E., exit Boulevard. The zoo is 1/2 mile on the right inside Grant Park. MARTA: Take bus #105 from West End station.

What's Fun In Atlanta?

PHOTO OPPORTUNITIES AT THE SWAN HOUSE

800 Cherokee Avenue S.E.
Atlanta 30325
404-624-1071
www.bcaatlanta.org

You've seen photos of the house, now see the house

The grand old house with its 26-acres of lush landscaping attracts more photographers than anywhere else in Atlanta. See why, but you'll want to bring your camera.

Built in 1928 by a weathy cotton broker, the house resembles an 18th-century English manor. The owner spared no expense. Considered a residential masterpiece.

Take the 45-minute tour of the house. (Purchase tickets at the Atlanta History Center.) All furnishings are original. Swans used as motifs earned the house its nickname. Your guide will point them out. Fun.

Hours

Tour

Mon. – Sat. .... 11 am – 4 pm
Sunday .... 11 am – 1 pm

Cost

Admission to the museum plus $1

Directions

In Buckhead. From Peachtree St. go west on W. Paces Ferry Rd. The Center is on the left. MARTA: Lenox Station; Bus #23 to Peachtree St./West Paces Ferry Rd. Walk 3 blks. west.

What's Fun In Atlanta?

RAFTING THE CHATTAHOOCHEE RIVER

Chattahoochee River National Recreation Area
1978 Island Ford Parkway
Atlanta 30350
770-399-8070
www.nps.gov

Where Deliverance was filmed

Over 2.9 million people find fun here every year. Most love to float the river.

This recreation area consists of 16 units along a 48-mile stretch of the Chattahoochee River. The area provides hiking, fishing, picnicking, and boating.

Water ranges from Class II to Class IV rapids. From the park's **Johnson Ferry and Power Island Outlet** rent boats starting weekends in May. Trips take 2 to 5 hours. An additional fee is charged for shuttle service, 770-395-6851.

The following private outfitter rents kayaks, canoes, rafts, and provide shuttle service: **the Chattahoochee Outdoor Center,** 1990 Island Ford Parkway, Atlanta, 30350, 770-395-6851.

The park's headquarters is open daily from dawn to dusk. No entrance fee. Parking $2. Friendly rangers offer any information you may need.

Directions
(Park's Headquarter's)

From GA-400, exit Northridge Rd. (Follow the signs to the park.) Follow Northridge Rd. onto Dunwoody Pl. Turn right onto Roberts Dr. and then right onto Island Ford Parkway.

What's Fun In Atlanta?

ROLLERBLADE PIEDMONT PARK

Skate Escape (rentals)
1086 Piedmont Avenue N.E.
Atlanta 30309
404-892-1292 Rental shop
404-875-8055 Visitor Center

Atlanta's fun park

Summers at Piedmont Park are great fun. Simply rent your in-line skates, bicycle, or skateboard from the little shop Skate Escape across the street. Then have an afternoon's blast at Piedmont Park.

The park features free symphony concerts, art festivals, and marathons.

It also hosts super popular annual festivals like the **Atlanta Dogwood Festival** in mid-April, 404-329-0501 and the **Atlanta Jazz Festival** in May, 404-817-6851.

The Atlanta Preservation Center offers historical walking tours of the park beginning at the park's Visitor Center, 404-876-2041.

Hours

Park	9 am – 6 pm
Rental Store (weekdays)	11 am – 6:30 pm
Weekends	11 am – 6 pm

Cost

Inline skate	$15/day or $5/hour
Safety gear	$1
Bicycles	($25/day) or $6/hour

Directions

In Midtown, at Piedmont Ave. and 12th St. MARTA: Midtown station. Walk to the park.

What's Fun In Atlanta?

RUN THROUGH THE FOUNTAINS AT CENTENNIAL OLYMPIC PARK

285 International Boulevard N.W.
Atlanta 30303
404-222-7275

World's Largest Fountains

Shaped like the five interlocking Olympic Rings, the fountains measure 85 feet long. Each ring is 25 feet in diameter. The moment is yours—run, jump, splash, and play all you want. Pretend you're at the Olympics.

Watch the water perform to lights and music daily at 12:30 pm, 3:30 pm, 6:30 pm, and 9 pm. Hear favorite tunes like *Coming to America*, the *1812 Overture Finale*, or *Chariots of Fire*.

This served as the gathering place for the 1996 Summer Olympic Games. The 21-acre park features an amphitheater and a reflecting pool.

Hours

Daily . . . . 7 am – 11 pm

Cost

Free

Directions

From Peachtree St., go east
on International Blvd.

What's Fun In Atlanta?

SHOP UNDERGROUND ATLANTA

50 Upper Alabama Street
Atlanta 30303
404-523-2311
www.underatl.com

Atlanta's biggest tourist attraction

Is it really underground? What do you think?

The shopping complex dates back to the 1800s when Atlanta was a railroad hub. Viaducts were built over the railroad tracks to solve this thriving area's congestion problem.

Comprises six city blocks with lots of quaint little shops, pushcart merchants, and food courts. Find everything from New York pizza to egg rolls. Street performers keep the atmosphere festive.

Stores and restaurants validate parking tickets for parking garages used along Martin Luther King, Jr. Boulevard.

If you're interested in the history of Underground Atlanta, the Atlanta Preservation Center offers walking tours, 404-876-2041.

Hours

Mon. – Sat. .... 10 am – 9 pm
Sunday .... Noon – 6 pm

Directions

The Kenny's Alley entrance is directly across from the World of Coca-Cola, between Martin Luther King, Jr. Dr. and Central Ave. MARTA: Entrance opposite Five Points station.

What's Fun In Atlanta?

STATE TROOPER OPENS THE GATE AT THE GEORGIA GOVERNOR'S MANSION

391 West Paces Ferry Road N.W.
Atlanta 30305
404-261-1776

Georgia's governor invites you to his mansion

Visiting the Governor's Mansion begins with a state trooper's friendly greeting. He signs you in, then tells you where to park.

Now that you feel special, enter the 3-story mansion. The 30-minute tour is self-guided. A docent explains each room's significance, its history and furnishings.

The house contains one of the finest 19th century collection of Federal Period furnishings in our country.

Some highlights include a portrait of George Washington, a Benjamin Franklin vase, and a magnificant Italian chandelier at the front entrance.

Built in 1968, the Greek Revival mansion resembles a southern plantation house.

Hours

Tues. – Thurs. . . . . 10 am – 11:30 am

Cost

Free

Directions

In Buckhead, from Peachtree St., go west on West Paces Ferry Rd. The mansion is on the right. MARTA: Bus #40 (West Paces Ferry) from Lindbergh station.

What's Fun In Atlanta?

TASTE THE WORLD OF COCA-COLA ATLANTA

55 Martin Luther King, Jr. Drive
Atlanta 30303
404-676-5151

Home in Atlanta

Over nine million visitors come here annually. One of Atlanta's biggest attractions. See why.

A self-guided tour explores the world's most popular soft drink's history, beginning in Atlanta.

See clips of 45 years of advertising. Over 1000 artifacts on display. Watch a 10-minute presentation on their production and distribution system. Inspiring.

Coke sells in over 200 countries. Sample as many as 22 exotic soft drinks sold in countries like Japan, Thailand, Mexico, and Mozambique.

And then there's the store, loaded with in Coca-Cola merchandise. Your friends will want to know where you bought your cool stuff.

Open until 6 pm in the summer. A must-do.

Hours

(Closed Thanksgiving, Christmas Eve/Day, New Year's Eve/Day)

Mon. – Sat .... 9 am – 5 pm
Sunday .... Noon – 6 pm

Cost

Adults $6
Children 6-11 .... $3
Seniors 55+ $4

Directions

On Martin Luther King, Jr. Dr. at Central Ave. MARTA: Five Points station.

What's Fun In Atlanta?

THE "HOT" SIGN AT KRISPY KREME DONUTS

295 Ponce de Leon Avenue
Atlanta 30308
404-876-7307
www.krispycreme.com

World's most beloved donut

When the HOT sign lights up, passersby know it is time to pull over for freshly-made donuts.

What's the fuss? Freshly-made Krispy Kremes literally melt in your mouth. You will ooh and ahh at the first bite.

This Atlanta institution has satisfied the locals' craving for tasty donuts since 1964, making over 1200 dozen donuts an hour and over 8 million dozen a year.

Although the yummy flavors include chocolate iced, lemon filled, and devils food, the glazed donut is by far the most popular.

Many order their donuts with a diet coke? Hey, there're so good, if you have to justify the calories, it's ok.

Other location:
806 Ralph D. Abernathy Boulevard S.W.
404-758-6868

Hours

Open 24 hours

Cost

1 glazed donut	65 cents
1 dozen donuts	$4.29

Directions

On Ponce de Leon Ave. at Piedmont St.

What's Fun In Atlanta?

TOUR THE FOX THEATRE

660 Peachtree Street N.E.
Atlanta 30365
404-881-2100
404-876-2040 Tours

Atlanta's exotic 1920s theater

The Fox Theatre—the rage of its day.

Saved from the wrecking ball in the 70s. Now completely restored, the Fox Theatre thrives again with Broadway shows, operas, concerts, ballets, and film festivals performing almost every night.

Only a few theaters like this still remain. This old majestic movie palace is now on the National Register of Historic Places.

Take the tour that lets you see it all, including the fabulous Egyptian ballroom. You'll be surprised. Offered by the Atlanta Preservaton Center.

Not recommend for children under 8 years of age. Scheduled events may cancel a tour. Call before going.

Hours

Tours

Mon.–Thur. .... 10 am
Saturday .... 10 am & 11 am

Cost

Adults $5
Seniors/Students $4

Directions

On Peachtree St. at Ponce de Leon St. MARTA: Adjacent to the North Ave. station.

What's Fun In Atlanta?

TOUR THE GEORGIA DOME

One Georgia Dome Drive N.W.
Atlanta 30313
404-223-8687 or 404-223-9200

World's largest cable-supported dome

The Georgia Dome—home of the Atlanta Falcons—is considered one of the finest football stadiums in the country.

The dome enables Atlanta to host the Super Bowl, basketball championships, and the Chick-Filet-A Peach Bowl.

You don't even have to be a sports fan to be impressed. Costing $217 million, the dome has state-of-the-art everything. It seats 71,594 people. The roof weighs only 68 pounds.

And here's your chance to really see it. Take the 45-minute tour. Although tours are for groups of 15 or more, you can join in.

Not recommended for children under age 3. Scheduled events sometimes cancel tours. Call for reservations before going.

Hours
(Tours start on the hour)

Daily . . . . 10 am – 4 pm

Cost

Adults $2
Students/Seniors $1
Children 3 – 12 . . . . $1

Directions

From Peachtree St., turn east on International Blvd. MARTA: Exit at Omni & Vine City station on westbound line.

What's Fun In Atlanta?

UNCLE REMUS STORIES AT WREN'S NEST

1050 Ralph David Abernathy Blvd.
Atlanta 30310
404-753-7735

Storytellers make the author's home rock

What better place to hear the tales of Uncle Remus than in author Joel Chandler Harris's home, called the Wren's Nest. Call for the storytellers' schedule.

At age 13, Harris worked as an apprentice for the quarterly plantation newspaper, *The Countrymen*. While living out in the countryside he became interested in the slaves' storytelling. Later on, he would recall these stories in his editorials and create the character Uncle Remus.

Harris often wrote sitting in his wicker rocking chair on his porch. His home was an 1870s farmhouse that later in 1884 was given a Queen Ann Victorian facade. Many of the furnishings are original. See old family photos, first edition books, and his typewriter. The tour includes a slide presentaion about his life.

Hours (Group Tours)
Tues. – Sat. .... 10 am – 2:30 pm
Tours on the hour
Tues., Thurs. & Sat. .... 10 am & 2:30 pm
Cost (Individual rates)
Adults $7
Seniors/Students ages 13 – 19 .... $6
Children ages 4 – 12 .... $4

Directions
From I-20W, exit Ashby St. Go left on Ashby St. then right on Ralph Abernathy Blvd. Two blks. down on the left. MARTA: West End Station, take bus #71.

What's Fun In Atlanta?

VIEW ATLANTA ATOP THE WESTIN PEACHTREE PLAZA HOTEL

Sun Dial View
210 Peachtree Street
Atlanta 30303 404-589-7506

Here's how to see Atlanta

On a clear day, see Stone Mountain from atop the Westin Peachtree Plaza Hotel. The tallest hotel in the Western Hemisphere. Absolutely breathtaking.

From the lobby, take the glass elevators to the 73rd floor—the Sun Dial View—just below the Sun Dial Restaurant.

If you order from either the bar or the restaurant, the ride up is free. Reservations required for the restaurant.

It takes 1 hour for the observation deck to make a revolution.

Hours

Elevator ride to view	10 am – 11 pm
Daily (Lunch)	11:30 am – 2:30 pm
Daily (Dinner)	6 pm – 11 pm

Cost

(Elevator ride to the top)

Adults	$7.50
Children 4-12	$4
Children under 4	Free
Seniors 55+	$4

Directions

Downtown. Peachtree St. and International Blvd. MARTA: Peachtree Center station.

What's Fun In Atlanta?

VISIT THE NEWLY RESTORED STATE CAPITOL BUILDING

Capitol Avenue
Atlanta 30334
404-656-2844
www.sos.state.ga.us

Now in its 1889 grandeur

After chipping away layers of paint and wallpaper, the State Capitol Building looks like it did in 1889.

Although there's a 45-minute tour offered several times a day, it's just as fun to explore on your own. (Ask for a self-guiding brochure at the front desk.)

Highlights include the magnificent grand stairways, the 237-foot rotunda, the oldest portraits in Georgia (located in the rotunda area), and, oddly enough, the museum's 2-headed snake. (Only in Georgia, right?)

History buffs love to see the flag collection on the 1st floor.

Outside, Miss Freedom sits atop the 75-foot dome. Frequently struck by lightning, the 15-foot, 2000-pound statue often requires a new torch.

If you park in nearby state-owned lots, parking is only $3.

Hours

Mon. – Fri. . . . . 8 am – 5 pm
Tours . . . . 10 am, 11 am, 1 pm, & 2 pm

Cost

Free

Directions

On Capitol Ave. between MLK Jr. Dr. and Mitchell St. MARTA: Georgia State station.

 *What's Fun In Atlanta?*

WHO'S WHO AT THE OAKLAND CEMETERY

248 Oakland Avenue S.E.
Atlanta 30312, 404-688-2107

Sightsee this fascinating old cemetery

An old Victorian cemetery of Atlanta's who's who. Thousands come to find the grave of Margaret Mitchell, the famous author of *Gone With The Wind*. It's not unusual to find souvenirs left on golf celebrity Bobby Jones's tombstone.

Confederate soldiers and generals, former governors, and even Union soldiers are buried here.

Discover why two dogs and a mockingbird named Tweet are here too. The stories told are fascinating.

Take the tour or pick up the self-guiding brochure for $1. Either way is lots of fun. The cemetery's a haven for phenomenal art, history, and architecture.

Hours

(Cemetery)

Daily Office .... 9 am – 5 pm
Guided tours (March – November, except holidays)
Saturday (Sunday 2 pm) .... 10 am & 2 pm

Cost

(Guided tours)

Adults (Children $1) $5
Students/Seniors $3

Directions

From I-20E., take #59A (the 1st exit off I-75/I-85). Turn left (north) on Boulevard, then left on Memorial Dr. Turn right on Grant St. and right at the stop sign to enter the gates. MARTA: King Memorial station. Walk south on Grant St. to MLK Dr.

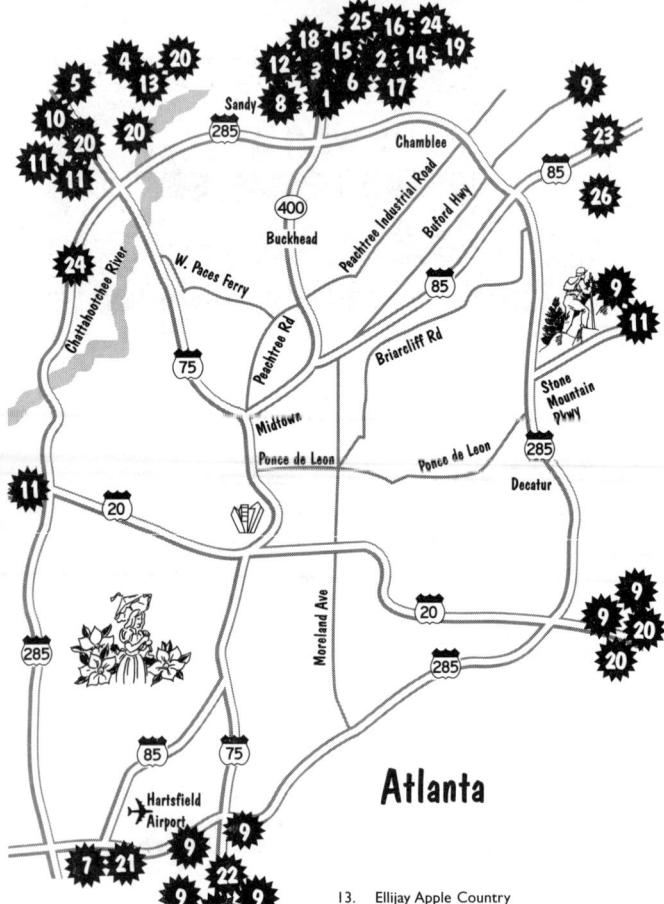

Atlanta

Locations:
1. Amicalola Falls State Park
2. Anna Ruby Falls
3. Appalachian National Scenic Trail
4. Blue Ridge Railroad
5. Brasstown Bald
6. Burt's Pumpkin Farm
7. Callaway Gardens
8. Chattahoochee Nature Center
9. Christmas Tree Farms
10. Cloudland Canyon State Park
11. Covered Bridge Trail of Georgia
12. Day Hikes on the Appalachian Trail
13. Ellijay Apple Country
14. Guided Fishing Trips
15. Horseback Riding in the Mountains
16. Kayaking, Canoeing, Tubing and Rafting Outfitters
17. Lake Lanier Islands Resort
18. Mountain Biking
19. Panning for Gold
20. Pick-Your-Own-Fruit Farms
21. Pine Mountain Wild Animal Park
22. Scenic Drives
23. Tallulah Gorge State Park
24. Unicoi State Park and Lodge
25. Vogel State Park
26. Yellow River Wildlife Game Ranch

Chapter 2
THE GREAT OUTDOORS
Parks, Recreation, Day Trips, Nature & Scenic Drives

Amicalola Falls State Park	44
Anna Ruby Falls	45
Appalachian National Scenic Trail	46
Blue Ridge Railroad	47
Brasstown Bald	48
Burt's Pumpkin Farm	49
Callaway Gardens	50
Chattahoochee Nature Center	51
Christmas Tree Farms	52
Cloudland Canyon State Park	53
Covered Bridge Trail of Georgia	54
Day Hikes on the Appalachian Trail	55
Ellijay Apple Country	56
Guided Fishing Trips	57
Horseback Riding in the Mountains	58
Kayaking, Canoeing, Tubing, and Rafting Outfitters	59
Lake Lanier Islands Resort	60
Mountain Biking	61
Panning for Gold	62
Pick-Your-Own-Fruit Farms	63
Pine Mountain Wild Animal Park	64
Scenic Drives	65
Tallulah Gorge State Park	66
Unicoi State Park and Lodge	67
Vogel State Park	68
Yellow River Wildlife Game Ranch	69

The Great Outdoors

AMICALOLA FALLS STATE PARK

240 Amicalola Falls State Park Road
Dawsonville 30534
706-265-4703 Park
800-573-9656 Reservations

Georgia's highest waterfall

Amicalola means "tumbling waters" in Cherokee.

Water spills 729 feet down the face of a steep rocky mountain. Climb along the trail at the base of the falls for a spectacular sight. Bring the camera.

A haven for hikers. The park's 8-mile approach trail takes you to Springer Mountain, the beginning of the 2150-mile Appalachian Trail.

A fun thing to do! Spend the night in the mountains at this cozy lodge with the view, the (new) **Len Foote Hike Inn**. Only a 2 to 4 hour hike from the park. Enjoy a home-style dinner at 6:30 pm. Many stay here on their trek to Maine. Others just like to stay here.

An overnight stay costs $65/person for double occupancy including meals. Trail lunches available for an additonal charge, 770-389-7275 or www.hike-inn.com.

Hours

Park (daily) .... 7 am – 10 pm
Park Office .... 8 am – 5 pm

Cost
(Park)

Entrance fee .... $2 per car
Wednesdays .... Free

Directions *(85 miles from Atlanta)*

Amicalola State Park 15 miles northwest of Dawsonville on Hwy. 52.

The Great Outdoors

ANNA RUBY FALLS

Chattooga Ranger District
Burton Road, Highway 197
Clarkesville 30523
706-878-3574

Worth the drive

Two falls in one, twice the fun. See where two waterfalls tumble together down the face of Tray Mountain—the York Creek on the left and Curtis Creek on the right. Bring the camera.

Hike the easy to moderate .4-mile hike to the base of the double falls.

Anna Ruby Falls is a 1600-acre scenic area. The 4.6-mile Smith Creek hiking trail connects the area with Unicoi State Park. A popular hiking trail.

Stop in at the visitor center. Gift shop.

Hours

Visitor center closed Tuesdays and Wednesdays during the winter

Visitor center (daily, summer) . . . . 10 – 5 pm
Park (daily, summer) . . . . 9 am – 8 pm

Cost

Entrance fee . . . . $3 per car

Directions *(85 miles from Atlanta)*

From Helen, take GA 75 north for 1 mile. Turn right onto GA 356 and go 1.5 miles to the entrance. Turn left and go another 3.6 miles to the parking area.

The Great Outdoors

APPALACHIAN NATIONAL SCENIC TRAIL

Amicalola Falls State Park
240 Amicalola Falls State Park Road
Dawsonville 30534
706-265-4703

The Southern Terminus

The 2150-mile Appalachian Trail begins only 75 miles from Atlanta. Starting at Springer Mountain—the Southern Terminus—the trail crosses 14 states and ends at Mt. Katahdin in Maine.

Seventy-six miles of the Appalachian Trail run through Georgia, crossing into North Carolina at Bly Gap.

Hike to the Southern Terminus at Springer Mountain where the Appalachian Trail begins.

Pick the trail that's most appealing to you.

Leave your car at Amicalola Falls State Park. Hike the 8-mile approach trail to Springer Mountain. Serious hikers doing the Appalachian Trail use this approach. This trail is rigorous and it may require an overnight stay.

Or take the approach on FS 42 that crosses the Appalachian Trail. It's only 1/4-mile hike from the Springer Mountain parking area. From Highway 52 W. take the Nimblewill Road 2 miles to FS 28-1 (on the right). Go 2 miles to FS 77 (on the left). Take FS 77 for 5 miles to FS 42 at the top of the ridge. Go left on FS 42 for 2.7 miles and watch for signs.

The Great Outdoors

BLUE RIDGE RAILROAD

241 Depot Street, Blue Rigde 30513
800-934-1898 or 706-632-9833
www.brscenic.com

All aboard for fun

Only 90 miles from Atlanta. Ride this vintage steam train through the scenic Blue Ridge Mountains.

Catch the train in Blue Ridge city's old L&N Depot. Passengers choose to ride in air-conditioned coaches or open-air cars.

Bring along your picnic lunch. (Coolers must fit under your seat.)

The train lays over in McCaysville long enough to have lunch and explore the historic downtown. The round trip takes about 3 hours.

Make reservations well in advance. Have fun.

This railroad once was Georgia's main line. The last train through here was in the 1960s.

Hours

(Departures)

Fri. and Sat. . . . . 10 am – 2 pm
Sunday . . . . 2 pm
(Some) Mondays . . . . 11 am

Cost

Adults $24
Seniors $20
Children ages 3 – 12 . . . . $12
Premier class $30

Directions

From Atlanta, take I-75 N to I-575 N (it becomes Hwy. 515) all the way to Blue Ridge. At the traffic light (at the McDonald's), turn south towards downtown and then left on Depot St. Go one block.

The Great Outdoors

BRASSTOWN BALD

Brasstown Ranger District
1881 Highway 515, Blairsville 30512
706-745-6928 Office
706-896-2555 Visitors Center

On a clear day, see downtown Atlanta

Georgia's highest peak—Brasstown Bald—rises 4784 feet high. For a small fee, a van will drive you to the top. Otherwise, it's a steep .5-mile hike to the summit. (Take the van.)

Stop in at the visitors center on top of the mountain to watch the video presentation. Browse through the museum that tells about Georgia's gold rush days and the Trail of Tears. See displays on native wildlife.

The observation deck sits on top of the visitor center. Get a breath-taking view from all directions. Often the summer's haze obstructs the view. Spring and fall are great times to go.

You'll find the temperature on top of the mountain 10 degrees cooler than the parking lot. The park opens mid-April on weekends until Memorial Day. It stays open through November.

Hours

Daily .... 9 am – 5:30 pm

Cost

Parking $3/car

Directions

From Helen, take GA 75 north for 12 miles. Turn left onto GA 180 and continue for 6 miles to GA spur. Watch for signs.

The Great  *Outdoors*

BURT'S PUMPKIN FARM
4801 Highway 52
Dawsonville 30534
706-265-3701 or 800-600-BURT

Mountain farm raises pumpkins

Burt's Farm makes a sight in October. Take a hay ride through the pumpkin fields. Choose yours from thousands. Find pumpkins from $1 to $80. Fun thing to do with your family. Visit the "talking pumpkins."

The Country Store sells fresh-baked goodies, gourds, Indian corn, homegrown popcorn, and more. The farm opens daily from September 1 through October 31.

Make this a family Halloween tradition.

Hours
Call for times

Cost
Hay rides

Adults .... $4 per person
Children 1 - 12 .... $3

Directions
Half mile west of Amicalola State Pk. on Hwy 52.

The Great Outdoors

CALLAWAY GARDENS
Pine Mountain, 31822
706-663-2281

Hot spot for family outings/Christmas lights

Ahh . . . this is paradise. Lovely gardens. Claims to have the world's largest azalea garden. See endless varieties of wildflowers, depending on the time of year. Drive the 2.5-mile auto tour.

See the largest tropical conservatory—the **Butterfly Center**. Includes live butterflies and hummingbirds.

Most popular The **Discovery Center** offers a breathtaking view of Pine Mountain Ridge. Browse the unique galleries and gift shop. Full-service restaurant.

Rent bicycles; you'll find bike paths throughout the complex.

Come back for the holiday season. The drive-through holiday lights are a must-see.

Fun for day-trippers or family vacations. Facilities include a gun club, a championship golf course, tennis courts, fishing, fly fishing, and overnight accommodations.

Hours
Open 365 days per year (Hours are extended in the summer)
Daily .... 9 am – 5 pm

Cost
Adults ($12 on weekends) $10
Children 6 – 12 ($6 on weekends) $5
Seniors $10

Directions
Sixty minutes southwest of Atlanta. From I-85 and I-185, exit Highway 18. Watch for signs.

 *The Great Outdoors*

CHATTAHOOCHEE NATURE CENTER

9135 Wileo Road, Roswell 30075
770-992-2055, www.chattahoochee.com

For nature lovers

Tucked away, a refuge from city life. Explore the 127 acres of woodlands, ponds, and wetlands. Float the Chattahoochee River.

Guided nature walks for the whole family take place on Saturdays and Sundays at 1 pm and 3 pm. A naturalist gives special presentations on Sundays at 2 pm. Guided canoe trips also offered. Ask about their "Nature After Dark" program.

Also offers a wildlife rehabilitation center where the public can drop off injured wild animals.

Oh, to be a kid again. Popular place for children's birthday parties. Includes live animal demonstrations and a special birthday registry at the Nature Store. No pets allowed.

Hours

Mon. – Sat. . . . . . 9 am – 5 pm (8 pm summer)
Sunday . . . . Noon – 5 pm

Cost

Adults $3
Children 3 – 12 /Senior 60+ $1

Directions

From Atlanta, take GA 400 to exit #6. Bear to the right back over GA 400 and take an immediate right onto Dunwoody Pl. Follow 1.2 miles to Roswell Rd. Turn right at the 1st light after crossing the Chattahoochee River, then left onto Azalea Dr. At the 2nd light, turn left onto Willeo Rd. Go 1/2 mile.

The Great Outdoors

CHRISTMAS TREE FARMS

Catch the holiday spirit. Cut-your-own Christmas tree farms open after Thanksgiving and remain open through Christmas Eve. The following offer different varieties of trees. Some have hay rides, hot cider, cookies, and craft shops. Call for directions.

Berry's Christmas Tree Farm
90 Mt. Tabor Rd., Covington 30014, 770-786-1880

Bethany Tree Farms
606 Old Jackson Rd., McDonough 30252, 770-954-1665

December Farms
Santa's Trees & Craft Shop
4133 Old Cornelia Hwy., Gainsville 30501
770-869-7930

Hess Tree Farm
1574 Vasco Adcock Road, Monroe 30655, 770-267-9428

Homestead Christmas Tree Farm
3850 Hwy. 81 West, Hampton 30228, 770-707-0854

Jack's Tree Farms
P.O. Box 337, Bostwick 30623
706-342-1943 or 800-486-6733

Ridgeway Christmas Tree Farm
2962 High Falls Rd., Jackson 30233, 770-775-3120

Yule Forest
1220 Millers Mill Rd., Stockbridge 30281, 770-957-3165
www.yuleforest.com

The Great Outdoors

CLOUDLAND CANYON STATE PARK

122 Cloudland Canyou Park Road
Rising Fawn 30738
706-657-4050 Park
800-864-7275 Reservations

Scenic state park

This beautiful state park straddles a deep gorge. If you hike to the bottom of the gorge, you'll find two spectacular waterfalls. The falls flow over layers of sand and shale into lovely pools. (Groomed trail, less than a mile.)

From on top, the best view of the gorge is from the picnic area's parking lot. Bring your lunch.

The park has campsites, RV sites, and even backpacking campsites. Or stay in one of their 16 cozy cottages or the lodge that sleeps 40 people. Offers tennis and swimming.

Hours

Park (Daily) . . . . 7 am – 10 pm
Park Office (Daily) . . . . 8 am – 5 pm

Cost

Entrance fee . . . . $2 per car

Directions

Located on GA Route 136, 8 miles east of Trenton and I-59, and 18 miles west of LaFayette.

The Great Outdoors

COVERED BRIDGE TRAIL OF GEORGIA

225 LaChaize Circle
Atlanta 30327, 404-843-0018

See these classic old bridges, fun

In the 1820s, Georgia's covered-bridge builder—Ithiel Town—revolutionized bridge building with his "Town Lattice Truss."

Only 15 covered bridges still exist in Georgia; many are within 2 hours of Atlanta. Some were built by Ithiel Town. For a complete list of these bridges call 770-503-0800. Here are the four closest.

Concord

Built in 1872 (Town Lattice). Take I-75 north to I-285 west, exit #10, Symrna, 4 miles to Concord Rd. West 2 1/2 miles.

Euharlee

Built in 1888 (Town Lattice), 138 ft. long. Take I-75 north, exit #124, 8 miles southwest of Cartersville on Hwy. 113, 3 miles north on Euharlee Rd. 1/2 mile south of Euharlee.

Haralson Mills

Reconstructed in 1997 (Town Lattice), 150 ft. long. Take I-20 east, exit #40, Sigman Rd., to Hwy. 20 north, east on Bethel Rd., north on Haralson Mill Rd.

Stone Mountain Park

Built in 1891 (Town Lattice), 151 ft. long. Moved from Athens, GA. Take I-285, exit #30b, Hwy 78, 7.5 miles to park entrance.

The Great Outdoors

DAY HIKES ON THE APPALACHIAN TRAIL

DeSoto Falls Trail

The trail leads to 2 waterfalls along Frogtown Creek. Path runs .3 miles downstream, the other .75 miles upstream from the trail head.

Dockery Lake Trail

Trail makes a .5-mile hike around the lake with picnicking and fishing. Great for small kids. Located 9 miles north of Dahlonega on Hwys. 19/Ga 60. Take a right onto FS 654.

Gooch Gap to Woody Gap

A 3.5-mile hike with scenic views. Shuttle required. Trail starts on FS 42-1 from Highway 60 at Tritt's Store, 15 miles north of Dahlonega.

Lake Winfield Scott To Blood Mountain

Two trails from Lake Winfield Scott lead to Blood Mountain. Hike the Slaughter Gap Trail to the Appalachian Trail (2.7 miles) and then to Blood Mountain (1 mile). Return via Appalachian Trail and Jarrard Gap Trail (3.8 miles); makes a scenic loop.

Raven Cliffs Trail

A scenic 5-mile round-trip hike along Dodd Creek leads to a creek that plunges through a narrow grotto. Trail head is 3 miles north of Hwy. 75 near Helen on the Richard Russell Scenic Hwy.

Three Forks

Easy, scenic 3.1-mile hike from the parking area where the Appalachian Trail crosses FS 42 to the Three Forks area and FS 58. It's also worth hiking one mile further north to Long Creek.

The Great Outdoors

ELLIJAY APPLE COUNTRY

Gilmer County Chamber of Commerce
205 Craig Street, Suite 4
East Ellijay 30539
706-635-7400

Apple houses in the fall

Fresh-picked apples. Yum. Gilmer County, Georgia's apple capital, produces over 500,000 bushels of apples a year.

Apple houses open mid-August through mid-December. Some let you pick your own. Others celebrate the harvest season with hay rides and orchard tours.

Buy juicy, crisp apples, up to 20 different varieties, and a ton of apple products. You'll find apple cider, caramel apples, dried apples, apple bread, apple jelly, apple pie, you name it.

Then there's the **Georgis Apple Festival**. Held the 2nd and 3rd weekends in October at the fairgrounds south of Ellijay on Highway 5. Features live entertainment, lots of food, and hand-made arts and crafts.

Directions

From Atlanta, take I-75 N. Take the I-575 N/GA 5N exit # 268 towards Canton. Merge onto I 575 N. I-575 N become GA 5 N Follow to Ellijay.

The Great Outdoors

GUIDED FISHING TRIPS

Unicoi Outfitters
7280 S Main Street
Helen 30545
706-878-3083
www.unicoioutfitters.com

Catch a big one! Brown or rainbow trout up to 30 inches long or better. This outfitter stocks and maintains their own places to fish along the river.

Fish with or without a guide. Fishing with guides includes using gear. Costs $170 for a half-day and $275 for a full-day fishing with a guide. And $90 for a half-day and $150 for a full day without a guide.

Upper Hi Fly
Hiawassee
706-896-9075

Offers bass and trout fishing with an expert guide. Fish nearby Blue Ridge Lake, Lake Chatuge, or the Hiawassee and Nantahalia Rivers.

Guided fishing trips include lunch and fishing equipment. Popular times to fish are April, May, and June. Requires reservations as early as February. Costs $75 for a half-day and $150 for a full-day of fishing

The Great Outdoors

HORSEBACK RIDING IN THE MOUNTAINS

Gold City Corral
49 Forest Hills, Dahlonega 30533
706-867-9395
Offers horseback riding and chuck wagon cookouts. Located 4 miles east of the Appalachian Trail.

Sunburst Stables
3181 State Highway 255, Clarksville 30523
706-947-7433
Year-round 1-hour, 2-hour, and 3-hour guided trail rides in the Chattahoochee National Forest, $20/hour per person.

Trackrock Stables
4890 Trackrock Campground Road
Blairsville 30512, 706-745-5252
Offers 1-hour and 2-hour guided trail rides at $20/hour per person.

Sunny Farms North
1332 Longbranch Road, Dahlonega
706-867-9167
By reservation only. Unguided trail rides in the mountains. Costs $20 per horse. Open all year.

The Great Outdoors

KAYAKING, CANOEING, TUBING AND RAFTING OUTFITTERS

The scenic rivers, the Chattahoochee River, the Chestatee, and the Etowah offer miles of fun family recreation. These friendly outfitters offer float trips down these rivers that include shuttle service. Depending on the water conditions, beginners are welcome.

Appalachian Outfitters
Highway 60
Dahlonega 30533
706-864-7117 or 800-426-7117

Broad River Outpost
112 Witcher Road
Carlton 30627, 706-795-3242

Go with the Flow
4-A Elizabeth Way
Roswell 30075, 888-345-FLOW

River Right Outfitters
122 Advanture Trail
Ellijay 30540, 706-635-2524

Southeastern Expeditions
50 Executive Park South Suite 5016
Atlanta 30329, 404-329-9433

Wildwood Outfitters
7272 South Main Street
Helen 30545, 706-865-4451

The Great Outdoors

LAKE LANIER ISLANDS RESORT

6950 Holiday Road
Lake Lanier Islands 30518
770-932-7200

Hot spot for summer fun

The main attraction—the water park—draws thousands every year. So do the white sandy beaches.

But that's not all this 1200-acre island resort has to offer. There are tons of things to do.

Rent sail boats, ski boats, houseboats, paddle boats, and canoes. Ride horseback along the shore line, ride bikes through the woods, play tennis and golf.

The resort offers lakefront rental houses, camping, and two resort hotels: the Lake Lanier Islands Hilton and the Stouffer Renaissance.

Come back during the holidays for the **Magical Night Lights,** a six-mile, drive-through light show. Bring your family and friends. Admission for a carload is $25. Call for details.

Hours for the water park
(Open weekends May – Sept., Memorial Day – Labor Day)

Mon. – Fri. . . . . 10 am – 6 pm
Sat. –Sun. . . . . 10 am – 7 pm

Cost (Water Park)

Adults . . . . $25.67 (with tax)
Children over 42 in. . . . . . . $17.17 (with tax)
Children under 2 . . . . Free

Directions

From Atlanta, take I-85 to exit #45. Continue on I-985 to exit #1. Turn left at the end of the ramp. Follow the signs.

The Great **Outdoors**

MOUNTAIN BIKING

www.dahlonega.org

Enjoy fun mountain biking trails in the Chattahoochee National Forest.

Rent mountain bikes in Dahlonega at the **Mountain Adventures Cyclery**, located on Clayton Drive, 706-864-8525. The shop will advise you on trails that your skill level, including easy ones for those who have never done this before.

Three popular mountain biking trails include Bull Mountain, Turner Creek, and Jake Mountain. To get to these trails, take Highway 52 W 8 miles outside Dahlonege to Nimblewill Church Road. The trails are located off 28-1, two miles on the right.

Bull Mountain Trail

Most popular and accessible trail. Makes an 11-mile loop. Very scenic. From Nimblewill Church Road, go right .3 miles on FS 28-1 and turn left on FS 83. Go 2 miles to bike parking areas. (Difficult)

Turner Creek Trail

To reach this trail on Wahsega Rd., Go 3.7 miles on FS 28-1 to Turner Creek. The trail is on the right. (Moderate)

Jake Mountain Trail

The parking lot for this trail is located off Nimblewill Church Road, on the right, between Hwy 52 and FS 28-2. (Difficult)

 *The Great Outdoors*

PANNING FOR GOLD

Gold fever still lingers in Lumpkin County.

Panning for gold remains a popular pasttime. Strike it rich? Have fun trying.

Consolidated Gold Mines

185 Consolidated Gold MIne Road
Dahlonega, GA 30533, 706-864-8473
Offers a tour of a real historic gold mine
that includes panning for gold.

Crisson Gold MIne

2736 Morrison More Parkway
Dahlaonega, GA 30533
706-864-6363
Open daily, year-round. Pan for gold and mine
for gemstone mining. Families welcome.
Indoor panning in the winter.

Gold'N Gem Grubbin

75 Gold Nugget Lane
Cleveland, 30528
706-865-5454
Grubbing for gems and hunting for gold, year-round. All activities are outdoor.
Jewelry making on site. Also camping,
fishing, RV hookups.

The Great Outdoors

PICK-YOUR-OWN-FRUIT FARMS

Make this one of your favorite family outings. Call for directions and what's in season.

Berry Patch Farms
786 Arnold Mill Rd., Woodstock 30188, 770-926-0561
(Blueberries, pumpkins, and Christmas trees)

The Blueberry Farm
1363 Hwy. 151, LaFayette 30728, 706-638-0908
(Blueberries)

Futral Farms Peach Orchard
5061 Jackson Rd., Griffin 30223, 770-228-1811
(Peaches)

Hillcrest Orchards (Apple House)
9696 Hwy. 52, East Ellijay 30540, 706-273-3838
(Apples, strawberries, and peaches)

Open Air Orchards
1414 Dallas Hwy., Villa Rica 30180, 404-355-1870
(Blueberries, blackberries, and peaches)

Thomas Orchards & Greenhouse
6091 Macon Hwy., Bishop 30621, 706-769-5011
(Peaches, plums, nectarines, and pecans)

The Great Outdoors

PINE MOUNTAIN WILD ANIMAL PARK

1300 Oak Grove Road
Pine Mountain 31822
706-663-8744, www.animalsafari.com

A drive-through and walk-through zoo

The owners, after traveling the world, decided to open a wild animal park in Georgia.

Now a reality, the park offers animals from far-off places like Africa, India, Australia, Europe, South America, North America, and even the North Pole.

Wind through 3.5 miles of natural setting filled with exotic animals. The drive-through tour takes about an hour.

Visit Old McDonald's Farm, a walk-through zoo. Visit the Monkey House, the Alligator Pit, the Petting Zoo, the Tropical Bird House, and the Georgia Wildlife Museum.

Picnicking areas and concessions. See the new African Room and gift shop.

Hours
(Closed Christmas)

Daily .... 10 am – closing time seasonal

Cost
(Admission varies with season--call before going)
Summer only

Adults $12.95
Students/Seniors 60+ $11.95
Children ages 3 – 9 .... $9.95
Children under 3 .... Free

Directions (87 miles from Atlanta)

Take I-85 S to Exit 21. Take I-185 S to exit 42. Turn left and go 6.7 miles and turn right on Oak Grove Rd. The park is 2 miles on the left.

The Great Outdoors

SCENIC DRIVES ALONG MOUNTAIN HIGHWAYS AND BACKROADS

Peach Blossom Trail

Scenic drive into peach country and the setting for Margaret Mithell's famous novel *Gone With The Wind*. Peach trees bloom in March. Peaches from mid-May through mid-August. You'll pass many pick-your-own farms. Follow US 41/341, Jonesboro to Perry (100 miles).

Richard Russell Scenic Highway

Scenic 38-mile loop in Blue Ridge Mountains with specacular views of Brasstown Bald, Georgia's highest peak and Dukes Creek Falls. Follow 17/75, SR 180, SR 348, and Alt. SR 75.

Ridge Valley Scenic Byway

A national scenic byway through the Chattahoochee and Oconee National Forests. Makes a 47-mile loop beginning at Highways 136 and 201 in Villanow. Pass Keown Falls Scenic Area—waterfalls and wildlife. Plenty of scenic ridges and valleys to view. Follow SR 136, to Furnace Creek Rd. to Pocket Rd., to Johns Creek Rd. to Floyd Springs Rd., to US 27, to Thomas Ballenger Rd. and to East Armuchee Rd.

Scenic Georgia Highway 197

From GA-197 past Highway 365, take a 50-mile stretch of winding road heading north towards US 76. Be prepared for dips and turns as the road follows the Soque River. Small craft shops dot the sides of the road. Pass Moccasin Creek State Park. Stop for lunch at family-owned La Prada's Restaurant.

The Great Outdoors

TALLULAH GORGE STATE PARK

P.O. Box 248
Tallulah Falls 30573
706-754-7970 Park
800-864-7275 Reservations

Scenic gorge with interpretive center

See one of the most spectacular gorges in the eastern U.S. The gorge runs 2 miles long and nearly 1500 feet deep.

Obtain a free permit from the visitor center to hike the gorge. Only 100 people allowed a day.

Or stop at the gorge overlook, watch for the sign that leads to the Scenic Loop along Old Highway 441.

The state-of-the-art interpretive center features an award-winning film. The presentation takes you on a journey through the gorge. See this.

If you like mountain biking, the park offers over 20 miles of paved trails.

Campsites, fishing, picnicking, and swimming.

Hours

Park (Daily) .... 8 am – dark
Park Office .... 8 am – 5 pm

Cost

Parking fee .... $4 per car

Directions

From Atlanta, take I-85 N. Take I-985 N/Lanier Pkwy exit #113 towards Gainsville. Then take US-23N.

The Great Outdoors

UNICOI STATE PARK AND LODGE

P.O. Box 997
Helen 30545
706-878-3983 Park
800-573-9659 Reservations

One of Georgia's most beloved state parks

Lovely old state park with a 53-acre lake. A favorite for hiking, mountain biking, fishing, swimming, canoeing, tennis, and shopping. You'll find a terrific little arts and craft shop with beautiful (mountain) home-made quilts.

Stay in campsites, cottages, or the lodge that sleeps 100 people. Also a full-service restaurant.

Known for its outstanding programs, the park offers guided backpacking trips, fireside art and craft shows, a wildflower program, birding weekends, mountain concerts, photography, and astronomy.

Spend your next 4th of July celebration here—mountain style.

Hours

Park (daily) .... 7 am – 10 pm
Office (daily) .... 8 am – 4:40 pm

Cost

Entrance fee .... $2 per car

Directions *(88 miles from Atlanta)*

From Helen, travel 1 mile north on I-75 and go right on GA 356. The park is 2 miles down on the right.

 *The Great Outdoors*

VOGEL STATE PARK

7485 Vogal State Park Road
Blairsville 30512
706-745-2628 Park
800-864-7275 Reservations

One of Georgia's oldest and most popular

Beautiful Vogel State Park sits at the base of Blood Mountain in the heart of the Blue Ridge Mountains.

You'll find this a dandy place when the wildflowers are in bloom or when the leaves turn brillant red, yellow, and gold.

Crowded on weekends in the summer. Stay in campgrounds, cottages, or in primitive backpacking sites.

The amenities include a 20-acre lake, a swimming beach, picnic shelters, miniature golf, pedal boats, and a museum. Swimming, fishing, and hiking are favorite activites. The park's four hiking trails range in difficulty.

Annual events at the park include a Wildflower Program in April and Mountain Music Festival in September.

Hours

Summer

Daily .... 8 am – 10 pm

Cost

Entrance fee .... $2 per car
Cabins .... $75 – $85 per night
Campsites .... $8 – $15

Directions

3 miles north of Neel's Gap on US Hwy. 19/129.

The Great Outdoors

YELLOW RIVER WILDLIFE GAME RANCH

4525 Highway 78
Lilburn 30047
770-972-6643

Interactive, walk-through zoo

Friendly animals await your visit—or maybe the food you feed them. Either way, this fun, 24-acre walk-through petting zoo, located on the banks of the Yellow River, will be a winner with the kids.

Let the free-roaming animals like white-tailed deer, squirrels, rabbits, and chipmunks eat out of your hand. Other animals like the black bear, the buffalos, the raccoons, and the prairie dogs eat from their penned-in areas.

Summer is a popular time to see newborn fawns. Bring your camera.

Ask about their hayride parties.

Hours

(Last ticket sold at 5 pm)

Daily .... 9:30 am – 6 pm

Cost

Adults/Seniors $6
Children ages 3 – 12 .... $5

Directions

10 miles east of I-285 on Hwy. 78 East,
near Snellville, GA. Exit # 38B.

Locations:
1. Apex Museum
2. Alonzo F. Herndo Home
3. Bulloch Hall
4. Carter Presidential Center & Library
5. Center for Puppetry Arts
6. Dahlonega Gold Museum State Historic Site
7. Etowah Indian Mounds State Historic Site
8. Federal Reserve Bank of Atlanta's Monetary Museum
9. Fernbank Science Center
10. Georgia Music Hall of Fame
11. Kennesaw National Battlefield Park
12. Little White House State Park Historic Site
13. Rhodes Hall
14. Robert C. Williams American Museum of Papermaking
15. SciTrek
16. Southeastern Railway Museum
17. Tubman African-American Museum
18. William Breman Jewish Heritage Museum

Chapter 3
HISTORIC SITES & MUSEUMS

Apex Museum 72
Alonzo F. Herndo Home....................... 73
Bulloch Hall 74
Carter Presidential Center & Library 75
Center for Puppetry Arts 76
Dahlonega Gold Museum State Historic Site 77
Etowah Indian Mounds State Historic Site 78
Federal Reserve Bank of
         Atlanta's Monetary Museum 79
Fernbank Science Center 80
Georgia Music Hall of Fame 81
Kennesaw National Battlefield Park 82
Little White House State Park Historic Site....... 83
Rhodes Hall 84
Robert C. Williams American Museum
         of Papermaking....................... 85
SciTrek 86
Southeastern Railway Museum 87
Tubman African-American Museum 88
William Breman Jewish Heritage Museum 89

Museums And History

APEX MUSEUM

135 Auburn Avenue
Atlanta 30303
404-523-2739
www.apexmuseum.org

Black Americans celebrate their history

A new museum is in the works. It will mark the way into the Martin Luther King Jr. Historic District. Until then, this is still an important stop for history lovers.

Here's a small museum that focuses on African-American contributions in music, science, sports, and the arts.

Watch the videos and browse through the art gallery. See a vintage trolley once used on Auburn Avenue (King's prominent Black neighborhood) and a re-creation of Yates and Milton Drugstore (Atlanta's first Black pharmacy).

Hours

(Closed Thanksgiving, Christmas, and New Years)
Tues. – Sat. .... 10 am – 5 pm

Cost

Adult	$3
Students/Senior 55+	$2
Children under 4	Free

Directions

On Auburn Ave. at Courtland and Piedmont Sts.
MARTA: Take #3 bus to Peachtree St. from Five Points station.

Museums And History

ALONZO F. HERNDO HOME

587 University Place N.W.
Atlanta 30314 404-581-9813
www.theherndohome.org

This man's an inspiration

Born a slave, died a rich man. With only 2 years of education, Alonzo F. Herndo became Atlanta's wealthiest Black American.

First he owned a prominent barber shop. Then he founded the Atlanta Life Insurance Company. Both were successful businesses.

Tour his fantastic house. He and his wife designed it, then used the best Black craftsmen in Atlanta to build it.

After his death, his son Morris Bumstead Herndo took over the insurance business, building it to greater properity. See his fine art treasures throughout the house. All the furnishings are the family's.

This successful family helped support many Black community activities.

(Wednesdays, no admission charged; donations accepted.)

Hours
Tues. – Sat. .... 10 am –4 pm
Cost
Adults $5
Students $3
Directions

From I-20 West, exit Ashby St. and go north to Martin Luther King Dr. Go right, then left on Vine St. Continue to University Pl. Turn right. MARTA: Take the #3 bus Five Points station to MLK Dr. and Walnut. St. Walk up one-way street 1 block.

Museums And History

BULLOCH HALL

180 Bulloch Avenue
Roswell 30075
770-992-1731

President Theodore Roosevelt's mother's home

This beautiful old Greek Revival house has more significance than its period architecture. This was the home of President Theodore Roosevelt's mother, Mittie Bullock.

An early settler, Major James Stephen Bullock, built the house in 1840. Note the old trees around the house. Over a hundred of them are listed on the Historic Tree Register.

In 1853, Bullock's daughter held her wedding in the house.

The 45-minute tour takes you through the house. The surrounding buildings include the privy, the slave quarters, and the summer house.

Hours

(Tour are every hour beginning at 10 am; last one at 3 pm)

Mon. - Sat. . . . . 10 am – 3 pm
Sunday . . . . 1 pm – 3 pm

Cost

Adults/Seniors $5
Children ages 6– 16 . . . . $3

Directions

One block west of the historic town square. From GA-400, exit #6 and go west on Dunwoody Pl. to Hwy. 9. Go north to Hwy 120. Turn left. Then make a right on Mimosa Blvd. and a left on Bulloch Ave.

Museums And History

CARTER PRESIDENTIAL CENTER & LIBRARY

4411 Freedom Parkway
Atlanta 30307
404-331-3942
www.carterlibrary.galileo.peachnet.edu

Honors our 39th U.S. President

President Carter came from Plains, Georgia, but his Presidential Library's in Atlanta.

Learn about this great man's early life and his accomplishments as president. See photos, hear audio tapes, watch videos, and read important documents.

The most popular exhibits are the gowns belonging to many First Ladies, from Dolley Madison to Rosalynn Carter.

Enjoy the lovely Japanese gardens. Dining on the cozy cafe's patio offers a splendid view. Eat at the cafe without paying admission.

Hours

(Closed Thanksgiving, Christmas, & New Year's Day)

Mon. - Sat. .... 9 am – 4:45 pm
Sunday .... Noon – 4:45 pm

Cost

Adults $5
Children ages 16 & under .... Free
Seniors $4

Directions

From the north or south, take I-75/85 to exit 248C, Freedom Parkway. Follow the signs. MARTA: Take #16 Noble bus from Five Points station.

Museums And History

CENTER FOR PUPPETRY ARTS

1404 Spring Street, Atlanta 30309
404-873-3391
www.puppet.org

Even Kermit the Frog's been here

Puppet shows. Puppet-making classes.

Shows for all ages, including shows for grown-ups on Friday nights.

Puppet making classes are popular with adults and seniors too. Classes available Monday through Saturday.

The center houses an extensive collection of puppets from around the world. Tickets for performances also allow admission to the museum, so arrive at least 30 minutes before showtime.

Call for show schedule and make reservations in advance.

Hours

Daily .... 9 am – 5 pm

Cost (Show and Museum)

Adults $8
Children ages 2 – 18 .... $7

Museum only

Adults $5
Seniors/ Children (2 –13) $4

Directions

On Spring St. at 18th St. From downtown, take Peachtree St. to W. Peachtree. Go left on 18th St. MARTA: Art Center Station. Walk 2 blks. north on W. Peachtree St., then left on 18th to Spring St.

Museums And History

DAHLONEGA GOLD MUSEUM STATE HISTORIC SITE

1 Public Square
Dahlonega 30533
706-864-2257

1st U.S. gold rush

Gold seekers gathered into north Georgia 20 years before the 1849 Gold Rush in California. Between 1838 and 1861, more than $6 million in gold was coined in Dahlonega.

The former Lumpkin County Courthouse now houses interesting artifacts from the gold rush days. See gold nuggets and minted coins. A video explains what took place.

Dahlonega hosts several popular festivals. The World Gold Panning Competition takes place in April. The Wildflower Festival is in May, and the Dahlonega Gold Rush Days in October draws thousands, 706-864-3711 or 800-231-5543.

Hours

Mon. – Sat.	9 am – 5 pm
Sunday	10 am – 5 pm

Cost

Adults	$2.50
Children 6 – 19	$1.50
Seniors	$2

Directions

From Atlanta, take Hwy. 19/State Rd. 400 N. Take State Rd. 60 north into town.

Museums And History

ETOWAH INDIAN MOUNDS STATE HISTORIC SITE

813 Indian Mounds Road S.E.
Cartersville 30120
770-387-3747

Rare Indian ruins dating to 1000 A.D.

Only a few artifacts explain the Etowah Indian culture—they left no written record.

Six huge mounds, including a 63-foot earthen platform and a burial mound for nobility, make up the most intact Indian cultural site in the southeastern United States. Less than 10% of the site has been excavated.

Visit the museum. See the artifacts. Learn what they've discovered.

Hours
(Closed Thanksgiving, Christmas, & New Year's Day)
Tues. – Sat. .... 9 am – 5 pm
Sunday .... 2 pm – 5:30 pm

Cost
Adults $3
Children 6 –18 .... $2
Seniors 62+ $2.50

Directions *(45 miles from Atlanta)*

Take I-75 to Marietta/Chattanooga GA-113, exit #124 towards Catersville/Main St. Turn left onto GA-113 S. The highway then becomes GA-113/GA-61. Turn left of Etowah Dr. and then left onto Indian Mounds Rd.

Museums And History

FEDERAL RESERVE BANK OF ATLANTA'S MONETARY MUSEUM

1000 Peachtree Street
Altanta 30309
404-521-8764
www.frbatlanta.org

History of our U.S. banking system

It's a free museum that's all about money. Now located in its new facility.

Take the self-guided tour, see how currency was used throughout history. See a real gold bar. See coins minted in Dahlonega during the gold rush.

Watch a video on the U.S. Federal Reserve System. Established in 1913, it provides us with a sound currency and a healthy economy. Families welcome.

Guided tours are available by appointment only. No cameras allowed.

Hours

Mon. – Fri. .... 9 am - 4 pm

Cost

Free

Directions

Located on Peachtree St. and 10th St.

Museums And History

FERNBANK SCIENCE CENTER

156 Heaton Park Drive, Atlanta 30307
404-378-4311 www.fernbank.edu

Walk the forest, see a star show

Nature takes center stage. Walk the 65-acre forest trails, stroll through the water, vegetable, herb, and hummingbird gardens.

Take in a star show at the 500-seat planetarium. Call for show times and special holiday shows.

View the heavens with the 36-inch telescope, the world's largest for public use.

Inside, the museum houses dinosaur remains and exhibits on native birds . . . the Okeefenokee Swamp. See an Apollo 6 capsule.

Note: The forest opens Monday - Saturday from 2 pm - 5 pm. and on Sunday from 10 am - 5 pm.

The observatory opens for viewing any clear Thursday or Friday from 8 pm (dark) until 10:30 pm.

Hours

Tue. –Fri.	8:30 am – 10 pm
Saturday	10 am – 5 pm
Sunday	1 pm – 5 pm
Monday	8:30 am – 5 pm

Cost

Science Center .... Free

Planetarium

Adults	$2
Students (all ages)	$1
Seniors 62+	Free

Direction

From Ponce de Leon Ave. NE, turn left onto Artwood Rd., then right onto Heaton Park Dr.

Museums And History

GEORGIA MUSIC HALL OF FAME

200 Martin Luther King, Jr. Drive
Macon 31201
478-750-8555
www.gamusichall.com

Georgia's contributions to the world of music

Fun for music lovers. Over 450 Georgia musicians have contributed to jazz, country, classical, gospel, rock 'n roll, and rhythm and blues.

In their honor, the museum displays their instruments, performance outfits, photos, and other fascinating memorabilia.

The hands-on **Music Factory** allows kids to see themselves dancing on a big screen.

The **World of Music** plays songs in different musical styles. Hear what they sound like.

It takes 1 to 2 hours to see everything.

Hours

Mon. – Sat. . . . . 9 am – 5 pm
Sunday . . . . 1 pm – 5 pm

Cost

Adults $8
Children 4 – 18 . . . . $3.50
Children under 4 . . . . Free
Students/Seniors 60+ $6

Directions

From Atlanta, take I-75 S. towards Macon. Exit #165/I-16 E. towards Savannah. Take exit #2/US-80 and follow to MLK Jr. Blvd. Turn right.

Museums And History

KENNESAW NATIONAL BATTLEFIELD PARK

900 Dennesaw Mountain Drive
Kennesaw 30144
770-427-4686

Visit the famous battle sites

Not just any cannon sits on the visitor center's floor. This one was used in the Atlanta Campaign. The picture on the wall shows it on the battlefield. It's fun to be here when the cannon expert gives his talks. Call for times.

See a 20-minute video about what took place here and how it fits into the Atlanta Campaign. Then pick up a map for the auto tour at the front desk. Start at Kolb Farm where the fighting began.

Only buses drive to the top of the mountain on weekends (February through October). Buses leave every 30 minutes and are free.

If you're a Civil War buff, plan extra time for browsing through the bookstore. It carries numerous titles on every topic imaginable.

Hours

Park

Daily .... 7:30 am – dusk

Visitor Center

Daily .... 8:30 am – 5 pm

Cost

Free

Directions

From Atlanta, take I-75 N. and exit #269 towards Marietta. Follow the signs.

Museums And History

LITTLE WHITE HOUSE STATE PARK HISTORIC SITE

401 Little White House Road
Georgia Highway 85 Alt.
Warm Springs 31830
706-655-5870

U.S. President's country home

The house and its furnishings haven't change since Franklin D. Roosevelt lived here.

He built the house in 1932, just before his inauguration as President in 1933. He moved here hoping the spring waters of Warm Springs would cure him of polio. He claimed that the healing waters did help him.

Take the tour. You will see FDR's 1938 Ford convertible, fitted with hand controls so he could drive. See the Unfinished Portrait. President Roosevelt died from a massive heart attack while having his portrait painted.

See the collection of state stones and flags, the museum's array of personal items, home movies, and photos, and the treatment pools located nearby. Plan at least 1-1/2 hours to see everything.

Hours
(Closed Thanksgiving, Christmas, and New Year's Day)
Daily (last tour at 4 pm) .... 9 am – 4:45 pm

Cost

Adults 19 - 61 .... $5
Children 6 – 18 .... $2
Seniors 62+ $2
Children under 5 .... Free

Directions

Located 1/4 mile south of Warm Springs on GA Hwy. 85 Alt./U.S. Hwy.27 Alt.

Museums *And History*

RHODES HALL

1516 Peachtree Street N.E.
Atlanta 30309 404-885-7800
www.georgiatrust.org/rhodeshtml

Atlanta's castle

Amos G. Rhodes wanted his house to resemble the castles he saw in Europe. So he hired one of Atlanta's most prominent architects.

The house is the architect's crowning achievement and one of Atlanta's most significant landmarks.

Later on, developers intended to demolish the house for the land. But the Georgia Trust for Historic Preservation stepped in and saved it.

Today, the Trust maintains this treasure and uses it as their headquarters. It is listed on the National Register of Historic Places.

Take the tour. The house has one of Atlanta's finest late Victorian-style interiors.

But it's the carved mahogany staircase with the series of painted, stained-glass windows you must see. The windows make up one of the most remarkable Civil War memorials ever. Impressive. Beautiful.

Reservations required for groups of 10 people or more.

Tour Hours

Mon. – Fri. . . . . 11 am – 4 pm
Sunday . . . . Noon – 3 pm

Cost

Adults $5
Students/Seniors 60+ $4
Chidren under 5 . . . . Free

Directions

Parking may be difficult. On Peachtree St. between 15th and 16th Sts.

Museums *And History*

ROBERT C. WILLIAMS AMERICAN MUSEUM OF PAPERMAKING

500 10th Street N.W.
Atlanta, GA 30318, 404-894-5700

Everything about paper

Computers were expected to make us a paperless society, but today we consume more paper then ever.

Visit museum that explores the hard-to-live-without item, paper. Understand how paper was invented and how we process it in modern times.

Self-guided tours available. Guided tours must be scheduled in advance and cost $3 per person.

The museum offers a hands-on papermaking workshop as part of your guided tour. Ask for more details. This is only on Friday mornings and costs $5. Reservations required. Parking free.

Hours

Mon. – Fri. .... 9 am – 5 pm

Cost

Free

Directions

From I-75/85 N., exit #101 (Williams St./10th St.). Turn left on 10th St. From I-75/85 S, exit #102 (Techwood Dr./10th St.) Turn right on 10th St. MARTA: Take bus #37 or #12 from Midtown station.

Museums And History

SCITREK

395 Piedmont Avenue
Atlanta 30308
404-522-5500
www.scitrek.org

Atlanta's most popular family museum

Designed with fun in mind. Everything is hands-on. And it's not just for kids. Rated one of the top science museums in the country.

See live science demonstations. Visit Virtual Village. The museum offers touring exhibits from other countries.

Continue the fun browsing through the Science Store.

Hours

(Closed Easter, Thanksgiving, Christmas, & New Years)

Mon. – Sat. .... 10 am – 5 pm
Sunday .... Noon – 5 pm

Cost

Adults $7.50
College Students with ID $6
Children ages 3 - 17 .... $6
Seniors 55+ $6

Directions

Downtown Atlanta. From I-75 S., exit #249A Courtland St. Turn left at Harris St. (the 2nd light). Then turn left onto Piedment Ave. The museum is on the right. MARTA: Civic Center station. Walk 1 blk. south on West Peachtree St., then left on Ralph McGill Blvd. Walk 3 blocks east, left on Piedmont.

Museums *And History*

SOUTHEASTERN RAILWAY MUSEUM

3966 Buford Highway
Duluth, 30096
770-476-2013
www.srmduluth.org

Ride in a restored caboose

The collection of vintage railroad equipment is extensive. Includes Pullman cars and classic steam locomotives.

The museum focuses on the local history of the railway. Many of these old cars carried passengers from Atlanta to Key West, Florida.

Some of the cars even helped bring the Olympics to Atlanta.

Ride in the restored caboose pulled by a diesel locomotive around the track. Always a hit with the kids.

Hours

April – November

Saturday .... 9 am – 5 pm
Third Sunday .... Noon – 5 pm

December – March

Saturday (only) .... 10 am – 4 pm

Cost

Adults $6
Children 2 – 12/Seniors 65+ $4

Directions

Take I-85 N. of I-285. Exit #104 (Pleasant Hill Rd.). Follow for 25 miles. Turn right onto Buford Hwy. for 3 miles. Turn left on Peachtree Rd. Cross the railroad tracks and turn right into the parking lot.

Museums And History

TUBMAN AFRICAN-AMERICAN MUSEUM

340 Walnut Street
Macon 31201, 912-743-8544
www.tubmanmuseum.com

Georgia's largest African-American museum

If you're one for folk art, visit this museum. See world-class African art collections that include 2000-year-old Nok figures and carved ivory tusks.

The museum, created in honor of Harriet Tubman, focuses on African-American art, history, and culture in 14 different galleries.

See how Africans have influenced America in the Inventor Gallery, the Cooking Gallery, the Folk Art Gallery, the Local History Gallery, and the Mural Gallery.

Explore the history of the African-Americans from early days in Africa to the present in America.

Plan at least an hour to see everything,.

Hours

Mon. – Sat. . . . . 9 am – 5 pm
Sunday . . . . 2 pm – 5 pm

Cost

Adults $3
Children ages 3–12 . . . . $2

Directions *(80 miles from Atlanta)*

From I-75, take I-16 E. to exit #2, (Martin Luther King Jr. Blvd.). Turn right and cross the Otis Redding Bridge. At the 2nd traffic light, turn right on Walnut.

Museums And History

WILLIAM BREMAN JEWISH HERITAGE MUSEUM

1440 Spring Street N.W.
Atlanta 30309
404-873-1661

Jews in Atlanta tell their story

Discover a close-up-view of the Holocaust. Many surviving Jews live in Atlanta. Some migrated here from Russia. Hear their testimonies. Understand how they've influenced the Atlanta community.

Browse through the gift shop with its high quality art pieces. Visit the genealogy library and the galleries.

Many of the treasures (the diaries, documents, and photos) are over a century old. Items came from attics and basements of local Jewish residences.

Hours
(Closed Jewish Holidays)

Monday – Thursday	10 am – 5 pm
Friday	10 am – 3 pm
Sunday	1 pm – 5 pm

Cost

Adults	$5
Children/Students/Seniors 62+	$3
Children under 6	Free

Directions

Across from the Center for Puppetry. On Spring Street at 18th Street. MARTA: Arts Center Station. Walk 2 blks. north on W. Peachtree St. to 18th St., then left to Spring St.

Locations:
1. Actor's Express Theater
2. Agatha's A Taste of Mystery
3. Alliance Theater Company
4. Atlanta Ballet
5. Atlanta Broadway Series
6. Atlanta Opera
7. Atlanta Symphony Orchestra
8. Callanwolde Fine Arts Center
9. Hammonds House Galleries & Resource Center of African-American Art
10. High Museum of Art Folk Art and Photography Galleries
11. Jomandi Productions
12. King Plow Arts Center
13. Neighborhood Playhouse
14. Theater of the Stars

Chapter 4
THEATERS AND THE ARTS
Operas, Symphony, Live Theaters, and Visual Arts

Actor's Express Theater	92
Agatha's A Taste of Mystery	93
Alliance Theater Company	94
Atlanta Ballet	95
Atlanta Broadway Series	96
Atlanta Opera	97
Atlanta Symphony Orchestra	98
Callanwolde Fine Arts Center	99
Hammonds House Galleries & Resource Center of African-American Art	100
High Museum of Arts Folk Art and Photography Galleries	101
Jomandi Productions	102
King Plow Arts Center	103
Neighborhood Playhouse	104
Theater of the Stars	105

Atlanta Theater and the Arts

ACTOR'S EXPRESS THEATER

887 W. Marietta Street, Suite 7-107
Atlanta 30318
404-875-1606 Box office
www.actorsexpress.com

Appeals mostly to adults

If you like live performances that sing, here's your place. This theater's musicals and plays reach out to audiences' minds and souls.

Performs musical, cutting-edge, original, and classical plays. Have produced 9 world-premier plays. Offers shows year-round.

The 150-seat theater is located in the King Plow Arts Center—a piece of art in itself.

Order tickets online, by phone, or at their box office. Call for a performing schedule.

Hours
(Box office)

Wed. - Sun. .... 2 pm – 6 pm

Cost
$20 – $25

Directions

Coming south or north on I-75/85, exit the 10th St. exit. Go west on 10th St. until it dead ends. Turn left on Brady St. 2 blks. to Marietta St. Turn right. Cross the railroad tracks and make an immediate right to King Plow Arts Center entrance.

Atlanta Theater and the Arts

AGATHA'S A TASTE OF MYSTERY

693 Peachtree St. N.E.
Atlanta 30308
404-875-1610
www.agathas.com

Crime in Atlanta

Shows like *Who Wants to Murder a Millionaire? Death by Disco,* and *Holidays are Murder,* and you know this is serious fun stuff. All original shows.

Be a star! No scripts to memorize, no rehearsals. Arrive 30 minutes early for your part in the play. There's murder to solve.

What stage? The performance takes place around a tasty 5-course meal.

Reservations a must, with a deposit. Casual dress.

Hours

Mon. - Sat. . . . . 7:30 pm
Sunday . . . . 7 pm

Cost

Mon. – Thurs. . . . . $42. 40 per person
Fri. – Sun. $50

Directions

Half a block north of the Fox Theatre at the corner of Peachtree and 3rd Sts. MARTA: North Avenue station.

Atlanta Theater and the Arts

ALLIANCE THEATER COMPANY

Woodruff Arts Center
1280 Peachtree Street, Atlanta 30309
404-733-4600 Season tickets
404-733-5000 Box office
www.alliancetheater.org

Atlanta's leading theater company

Look no further than the Alliance Theater for excellent live theater for the whole family. Tops in every way—whether it's Shakespeare or locally written contemporary works.

Plays for all audiences. The Alliance Children's Theater is over 70 years old. Recent seasons now include the production *A Christmas Carol*.

Buy season or individual tickets. Purchase individual tickets by phone (includes a $3.25 handling fee) or at the Woodruff Arts Center's box office. Season runs from September through June and sometimes into the summer.

All performances are held at the Woodruff Arts Center. Over 350,000 people attend every year.

Hours
(Box office)

Mon. – Sat. .... 10 am – 8 pm
Sunday .... Noon – 8 pm

Cost
$21 – $27

Directions

At the corner of Peachtree and 16th Sts. in Midtown. MARTA: Arts Center station.

Atlanta Theater and the Arts

ATLANTA BALLET

1400 West Peachtree Street
Atlanta 30309
404-873-5811 Administraive Office
404-892-3303 (Ballet) Box Office
www.atlantaballet.com

Atlanta's on its toes

They dance, you dance. Not only does this ballet company give quality performances, but their Atlanta Ballet Centre teaches all kinds of dancing to anyone.

Since 1929, claims to be the oldest continually operating professional ballet company. Performs both classical and contemporary works. See them perform at the extravagant Fox Theatre.

And it just isn't Christmas in Atlanta without seeing the *Nutcracker*. A holiday tradition with many.

Their season features the Family Classic Theater with such favorites as *Peter Pan*. Purchase tickets through Ticketmaster, 404-817-8700, at the Fox Theatre's box office, 404-881-2100, or at the ballet's box office. (If tickets are purchased through the ballet, there's no handling fee.) The regular season runs October through May.

Hours

(Fox Theatre box office)

Mon. – Fri. . . . . 9 am – 6 pm
Sundays . . . . Noon – 6 pm

Cost

Individual tickets . . . . $25 – $45

Directions

Fox Theatre (660 Peachtree St. N.E.). On Peachtree St. at Ponce de Leon St. MARTA: Adjacent to the North Ave. station.

Atlanta Theater and the Arts

ATLANTA BROADWAY SERIES

www.broadwayseries.com
404-873-4300 Administration offices
800-278-4447 Season tickets
404-881-2100 Fox Theatre Box office

1st run Broadway shows in Atlanta

Atlanta loves Broadway. The city's high on the list for touring Broadway productions. Thanks to the Atlanta Broadway Series, Broadway hits—many blockbusters—come to Atlanta. All performed at the Fox Theatre.

Most tickets are purchased as season tickets for approximately six productions a year. Individual tickets are sold after that through Ticketmaster, 404-817-8700. Season tickets go on sale generally in March or April.

Hours
(Fox box office)

Mon. – Fri. . . . . 9 am – 6 pm
Sundays . . . . Noon – 6 pm

Cost
Individual tickets
$25 – $45

Directions

Fox Theatre (660 Peachtree St. N.E.). On Peachtree St. at Ponce de Leon St. MARTA: Adjacent to the North Ave. station.

Atlanta Theater and the Arts

ATLANTA OPERA

727 West Peachtree Street
Atlanta 30308
404-881-8801
www.atlantaopera.org

A night of opera at the Fox Theatre

Tickets can be hard to come by.

Atlanta loves opera. And Atlanta Opera produces the opera Atlanta loves. Considered one of the fastest growing opera companies in the nation.

Attend performances at the chic Fox Theatre. Four productions a year. Season runs April through October.

Subscribe. Individual tickets sold as low as $18 make opera-going affordable.

Students and seniors can purchase tickets at a 50% discount the day of a performance.

Purchase your tickets online, from Ticketmaster, 404-817-8700, located at Publix Super Markets, and at the Fox Theatre box office, 404-881-2100.

Hours

(Fox Theater box office)

Mon. - Fri. .... 9 am - 6 pm
Sundays .... Noon – 6 pm

Cost

(Individual tickets)
$18 - $126

Directions

Fox Theatre (660 Peachtree St. N.E.). On Peachtree St. at Ponce de Leon St. MARTA: Adjacent to the North Ave. station.

Atlanta Theater and the Arts

ATLANTA SYMPHONY ORCHESTRA

Woodruff Arts Center Symphony Hall
1280 Peachtree St., Atlanta 30309
404-733-4949 Concert Hot Line
404-733-4800 Season tickets
404-733-5000 Box office
www.atlantasymphony.com

One of our nation's top symphonies

Who says attending the symphony has to be stuffy? The Atlanta Symphony Orchestra offers such fun as *A Bark in the Park, Gospel Christmas, Halloween Hits,* and *Kid's Holiday.*

Performs over 200 times a year. Don't miss out on what they offer. Consists of the Masterworks, the Super Pops, the Family Concerts, the Holiday Concerts, and the Casual Concerts.

Summers are especially fun. Free concerts in Atlanta area park; most of them are held at Piedmont Park. Bring your blanket and picnic cooler.

Many rehearsals are open to the public. Come listen to them rehearse for a performance. Admission charged.

Hours

Mon. – Fr. .... 10 am – 8 pm
Sat. & Sun. .... Noon – 8 pm

Cost

$19 –$55

Directions

At the corner of Peachtree and 16th Sts. in Midtown. MARTA: Arts Center.

Atlanta Theater and the Arts

CALLANWOLDE FINE ARTS CENTER

980 Briarcliff Road, Atlanta 30306
404-872-5338
www.callanwolde.org

Atlanta's most active fine arts center

Coca-Cola heir Howard Chandler built a magnificent house. See the mansion on a self-guided tour. You'll marvel at the grand staircase, the walnut paneling, and the stained glass windows.

Enjoy browsing the wonderful art gallery, but call first for the exhibit schedule. Visit the art shop. Sign up for one of the many classes for adults and children. Offers classes in drama, painting, pottery, exercise, photography, and more.

And then there's the concert series. Attend a Sunday piano concert. Or listen to jazz out in the formal gardens. The Organ Society makes great use of the 3752-pipe Aeolian organ. Watch silient movies with organ accompaniment.

Come during the holidays. Local florists and interior designers have a heyday decorating the house. An annual fundraiser for the house, the event features gift and sweet shops.

Hours (Mansion)
Mon. – Fri. . . . . 9 am - 9 pm
Sat. & Sun (generally). . . . . 9 am – 3 pm

Cost
Free to tour house

Directions
From Peachtree St., turn east on 14th St. Go Right on Juniper St., and left on Ponce de Leon. Then left on Briarcliff Rd.

Atlanta Theater and the Arts

HAMMONDS HOUSE GALLERIES & RESOURCE CENTER OF AFRICAN-AMERICAN ART

503 Peeples Street S.W.
Atlanta, GA 30310
404-752-8730
www.hammondshouse.org

Works of African-American artists on display

The only focus here is African-American art. Located in a 19th-century Eastlake Victorian house, or simply the oldest house in the neighborhood.

See visiting and permanent collections. Wide diversity of artists. Houses a collection that includes Haitian art.

This national center dedicated to exhibiting and preserving African-American art is Georgia's only such museum.

Hours

Tues. – Fri. .... 10 am – 6 pm
Sat. – Sun. .... 1 pm – 5 pm

Cost

Adults $2
Students/Seniors/Children $1

Directions

From Ralph David Abernathy Blvd. Turn north on Peeples St. Go 2 blks. Art center's on the left.

Atlanta Theater and the Arts

HIGH MUSEUM OF ARTS FOLK ART AND PHOTOGRAPHY GALLERIES

133 Peachtree Street
Atlanta 30303
www.high.org
404-577-6940

Two popular forms of visual arts

Folk art's hot, so is photography. Find them both at the High Museum of Art's downtown location inside the 51-story Georgia-Pacific Center.

Enter at the street-level entrance on Dobbs Avenue or through the lobby on Peachtree Street.

The 2-story, award-winning museum offers gallery talks, films, and lectures as well as excellent traveling exhibits.

Hours

Mon. – Sat. .... 10 am - 5 pm

Cost

Free

Directions

Downtown at the corner of Peachtree St. and John Wesley Dobbs Ave. MARTA: Peachtree Center station.

Atlanta Theater and the Arts

JOMANDI PRODUCTIONS

675 Ponce de Leon, 8th Floor
Atlanta 30308
404-876-6346
404-870-0629 Box office
www.jomandi.com

Atlanta's Black theater has spirit

This is Georgia's largest and oldest Black-owned professional theater. See some of the finest African-American productions. Most of the shows are family oriented. Many of them go on tour.

Offering works of many great local and national playwrights. Produces 3 to 4 plays a year. Season generally starts in October.

Although plays are presented in theaters around town, most are held at the 14th Street Playhouse, 173 14th Street (at Peachtree St.). Call the box office for more details. Also purchase tickets through Ticketmaster, 404-817-8700.

Hours
(Box office hours depending on preformance schedule)

Cost
$12–$35

Directions

The 14th Street Playhouse is located on 14th and Juniper Sts., one blk. west of Peachtree St.

Atlanta Theater and the Arts

KING PLOW ARTS CENTER

887 W. Marietta Street N.W.
Atlanta 30318
404-885-9933

Art for Atlanta's sake

What was once an old plow and farm equipment factory now houses an art community. The old historic building makes its own work of art. Inside, find many early 1900 artifacts.

The local artists' gallery makes coming here fun Along with the gallery, you'll find a theater, Actor's Express, and a restaurant, the Food Studio, that serves dishes with an artistic expression. Serves dinner only.

Come for gallery shows and special events. Other findings here include art studios, and architecture and graphic art firms. Up above are loft apartments.

Hours

Daily .... 9 am - 9 pm

Cost

Free

Directions

Coming south or north on I-75/85, exit the 10th St. exit #84. Go west on 10th St. until it dead ends . Turn left on Brady St. 2 blks. to Marietta St. Turn right. Cross the bridge and make an immediate right into King Plow Arts Center.

Atlanta Theater and the Arts

NEIGHBORHOOD PLAYHOUSE

Decatur Arts Building
430 W. Trinity Place
Decatur 30030
404-373-3904
www.np.eventrunner.com

Family fun shows

Atlanta's best community theater. Offers plays with family appeal: Mainstream classical and contemporary works, all-time favorites.

Plays year-round. Purchase season tickets online, by phone 404-373-3904, or by mail.

Individual tickets available through the box office. Check their website for upcoming preformances. Box office opens 1 hour before show.

Box Office Hours

Mon. – Fri. . . . . 12:30 pm – 4:30 pm
Sat. . . . . 2 pm – 10 pm

Cost

Adults . . . . $16 and ($18 Sat.)
Students/ Children $12

Directions

Downtown Decatur. From downtown Atlanta, take Ponce de Leon Ave. to West Ponce de Leon Ave. Turn right onto W. Trinity Pl. Theater is behind the police station.

Atlanta Theater and the Arts

THEATER OF THE STARS

P.O. Box 11748
Atlanta 30355
404-252-8960
www.theaterofthestars.com

Summer theater's fun in Atlanta

Theater of the Stars brings Atlanta the best of Broadway—musicals and plays. Better yet, watch shows at the fabulous Fox Theatre.

See such performances as *Fiddler on the Roof, Phantom of the Opera,* or *Beauty and The Beast*. Offers about six shows a year, many family favorites.

Most shows take place during the summer months, but not always. Call for a performance schedule.

Season tickets go on sale as early as February or March. Buy individual tickets through Ticketmaster, 404-817-8700, or at the Fox Theatre box office, 404-881-2100.

Theater Box Office Hours

Mon. - Fri.	9 am - 6 pm
Sundays	Noon – 6 pm

Cost

Varies with performance

Directions

At the Fox Theatre. On Peachtree St. at Ponce de Leon St. MARTA: Adjacent to the North Avenue station.

Locations

1. American Adventures Amusement Park
2. Atlanta Beach at Clayton County International Park
3. Atlanta Motor Speedway Tour
4. Atlanta Rocks
5. Atlanta Walking Tours
6. Babyland General Hospital
7. Civil War Tours
8. Hot Air Ballooning
9. Ice Skating Rinks
10. Malibu Speedzone
11. Paintball Playing Fields
12. QZar Games
13. SailPlane Rides-Georgia Soaring Association
14. Six Flags Over Georgia
15. Skydiving
16. Thunder Road USA Georgia Racing Hall of Fame
17. White Water Atlanta

Chapter 5
AMUSEMENT PARKS, ATTRACTIONS, TOURS, EXTREME SPORTS, & MORE

American Adventures Amusement Park	108
Atlanta Beach at Clayton County International Park	109
Atlanta Motor Speedway Tour	110
Atlanta Rocks	111
Atlanta Walking Tours	112
Babyland General Hospital	113
Civil War Tours	114
Hot Air Ballooning	115
Ice Skating Rinks	116
Malibu Speedzone	117
Paintball Playing Fields	118
QZar Games	119
Sailplane Rides–Georgia–Soaring Association	120
Six Flags Over Georgia	121
Skydiving	122
Thunder Road USA Georgia Racing Hall of Fame	123
White Water Atlanta	124

Amusement Parks, *Attractions And More*

AMERICAN ADVENTURES AMUSEMENT PARK

250 Cobb Parkway
Marietta, GA 30062
770-424-9283

For the kid in everyone

If you're 12 years or younger, this place is for you. And it's open year-round.

All-time favorites: bumper cars, a mini roller coaster, a tilt-a-wheel, miniature golf, laser tag, and (best of all) go-carts.

There's even an itty-bitty Ferris Wheel, planes, a train, and a teacup twirl for little ones.

The Foam Factory is a popular attraction, especially if the weather's crummy. Over 50,000 foam balls delight kids. They climb, slide, dump, and shoot them from cannons. They even suck them up with a big vacuum. You can pay a separate admission just to play in the Foam Factory.

Hours

Open year-round, hours seasonal

Cost

(Fun Pass includes all rides)

Adults	$2.99
Children 4 - 17	$15
Toddlers	$4

Directions *(15 minutes from Atlanta)*

Take I-75 N and exit #265; follow the signs. Next to White Water Atlanta.

Amusement Parks, *Attractions And More*

ATLANTA BEACH AT CLAYTON COUNTY INTERNATIONAL PARK

2300 Highway 138
Jonesboro 30236
770-477-3766

Pretend you're an Olympian for the day

What was once the site for the 1996 Olympic Beach Volleyball Competitions now makes a fun place to take the family—a 200-acre recreation and water park.

Beach volleyball is still an attraction here, but so are the white sandy beaches that surround the spring-fed lake. There are paddleboats, water slides, and even a kiddie pool with smaller slides just for them.

And that's not all. The park's larger 13-acre lake makes a good family fishing hole—even if you're beginners. Bring along a picnic lunch; the facilities include picnic tables and pavilions.

Hours

Summer (Includes weekends May and September)
Mon. – Fri. . . . . 10 am – 6 pm
Sat. and Sun. . . . . 10 am – 8 pm

Winter (Park only)
Daily . . . . 8 am – 8 pm

Cost

(Winter, the park only is free)
Adults $6.95
Seniors/Children 3 – 12 . . . . $4.95

Directions

Take I-75 south. Exit #228 (GA-138) towards Jonesboro/Stockbridge.

Amusement Parks, Attractions And More

ATLANTA MOTOR SPEEDWAY TOUR

1500 Highway 19-41
Hampton 30228 770-707-7970
www.atlantamotorspeedway.com

American's hottest sport

It's awesome . . . you actually take a few laps around the track.

Get a behind-the-scenes look at this grand racing facility. The 30-minute tour includes pit road, the NASCR garage, and Victory Lane.

From a luxurious suite, watch a video on the past and future of auto racing. But the best part's at the end when they drive you out around on the track.

Don't miss Atlanta Motor Speedway and Winston Cup racing souvenirs in the gift shop.

Call for the racing schedule and tickets, 770-946-4211, or simply go online.

Hours

Tours begin every 1/2 hour, last tour at 4:30 pm

Mon. – Sat. . . . . 9 am – 5 pm
Sunday . . . . 1 pm – 5 pm

Cost

Adults $5
Children 7 – 18 . . . . $2

Directions

(30 miles south of downtown Atlanta)

Going south on I-75, take exit #235 (15 miles south) to U.S. Hwy. 19 & 41 S. Continue 15 miles.

Going north on I-75, take exit #205 (GA 16) and continue west through Griffin to U.S. Hwy. 19-41 N to Hampton.

ATLANTA ROCKS

1019-A Collier Road
Atlanta 30318, 404-351-3009
Other location:
4411-A Bankers Circle (Perimeter)
Doraville 30360, 770-242-7625

Try your skill at rock climbing

Beginners welcome.

At special times (Mondays, Saturdays, and Sundays at 4 pm) the experts instruct first-timers. You can be as young as five. Practically anyone can do it.

One of Atlanta's most exhilarating activities. The artificial terrain looks and feels like the real stuff—rocks. But the best part's the air-conditioning.

Shoes, harnesses, and belaying devices rent for $7.75. Or bring your own equipment. The second location's rates are cheaper.

Hours

Mon. Wed. & Fri.	3 pm – 10 pm
Tues. & Thurs.	11 am – 10 pm
Saturday	Noon – 8 pm
Sunday	Noon – 6 pm

Cost

Mon. – Fri.	$12.50
Sat. & Sun.	$14.50

Directions

From downtown Atlanta, take I-75 N to exit # 252B. Turn right onto Howell Mill Rd., then left onto Collier Rd.

Amusement Parks, *Attractions And More*

ATLANTA WALKING TOURS

The Atlanta Preservation Center
537 Peachtree Street NE
Atlanta 30308
404-876-2041 www.preserveatlanta.com

You haven't really seen Atlanta until you've seen the Egyptian ballroom atop the Fox Theatre . . . or visited the neighborhood of Civil Rights leader, Martin Luther King, Jr . . . . or toured the elegant Victorian homes of Inman Park.

Some of Atlanta's best, such as these places, were saved from the wrecking ball. Now you can explore them with a knowledgeable guide.

Walking tours include treasures like the historic downtown area, Druid Hills *(Walking Miss Daisy),* and Ansley Park.

All tours last from 1 to 2 hours, weather permitting. Call for schedule or check online. Reservations aren't required for groups of less then 15 people.

Tours lead by dedicated volunteers.

Cost

Adults $5
Students $4
Seniors $4

Directions

Meet at different places through of the Atlanta area.
Call or check online.

BABYLAND GENERAL HOSPITAL

73 W. Underwood Street
Cleveland, Ga 30528, 706-865-2171
www.cabbagepatchkids.com

Yup, the dolls keep coming

Cleveland, Georgia. What was once a quiet little town is now a tourist attraction. The Cabbage Patch Doll craze did it.

You know how popular these dolls were in the 80s. Now a 2nd generation of doll-lovers find their way here—where Cabbage Patch Babies are born every 30 to 40 minutes. And if you're the lucky one, you can name the baby and adopt it.

It's a free self-guided tour through the hospital, but don't think you won't be spending money. There's a gift shop loaded with all the Cabbage Patch Dolls imaginable. It's lots of fun.

Avid fans can bring their old dolls along for a cosmetic makeover; others want custom-made dolls to match own features. And wow! These dolls cost much more than the ready-made ones.

Hours
(Closed most holidays)

Mon. – Sat. . . . . 9 am – 5 pm
Sunday . . . . 10 am – 5 pm

Cost
Free

Directions

From Atlanta, take I-85E. to exit # 113; take GA-985N/365N to exit #24; take Hwy. 129 and travel 25 miles to Cleveland. Turn right on Underwood St.

Amusement Parks, *Attractions And More*

CIVIL WAR TOURS
2684 Canna Ridge Circle, N.E.
Atlanta 30345
770-908-8410
888-678-8942
www.civilwar-tours.com

Rent a historian for the day

Take along a historian. That way, you don't miss a thing.

Experts ride with you in your car on a tour of Civil War sites. If you like, design your own tour. This couldn't get more personal.

Groups of 6 or more get discounts. Children under 12 are half price.

Hours
Mon. – Sat. ... 9:30 am, 1:30 pm, 1pm – 5 pm

Cost
Per person .... $30 - $45

Directions
Meet at a designated place.

HOT AIR BALLOONING

Lawrenceville Adventures Aloft
P.O. Box 464246, Lawrenceville 30042
770-963-0149

See the countryside a whole new way. Open 7 days a week, year-round. Air time is an hour. But the ride also includes either a Continental breakfast or hors d'oeuvres with a champagne toast. First passenger $275, 2nd passenger $125. Call for reservations.

Marietta Atlanta Aerosports
125 Bascomb Drive, Woodstock 30189
770-928-4426

Early morning or sunset lift-offs, when the air is most stable. Fly over the Roswell-Alpharetta area. Requires 3 hours and includes a champagne celebration afterwards. Costs $200/person. Call ahead.

Snellville Balloon Safaries
2868A Lenora Road
Snellville 30039, 770-972-1741

Ride with the oldest hot air balloon company in Georgia. Open 7 days a week, year-round. Fly early mornings or 3 hours before sunset. Includes a champagne celebration at the end. Costs: 1st passenger $250 and $125 for each additional person up to 4 people.

Amusement Parks, *Attractions And More*

ICE SKATING RINKS

Ice Forum
2300 Satellite Boulevard
Duluth 30097, 770-813-1010

Cool spot for a hot day. Offers public skating sessions, group/private lessons, hockey, stick time, and birthday party packages (that can include lessons too). Call for hours.

Cost
2 Hours $6
Rentals $3

Directions
From I-85 ., exit #107. Take Duluth Hwy. 120. Go right on Satellite Blvd. Rink is on the right.

Other locations:
3061 Busbee Parkway
Kennesaw 30144, 770-218-1010
and
Mount Zion Blvd.
Jonesboro 30236, 770-477-5112

Parkaire Ice Arena
4880 Lower Roswell Road
Marietta 30068, 770-973-0753

Offers lessons as well as regular ice skating sessions. A popular area attraction for over 30 years. Call for hours and directions.

Cost
2 Hours $5
Rentals $3

Amusement Parks, Attractions And More

MALIBU SPEEDZONE

3005 George Busbee Parkway
Kennesaw, GA 30144
770-514-8081

Have a need for speed?

Here's how to hang out. A 12-acre race park with 4 tracks and arcade with over 100 of the latest games.

Drive their 300 horsepower dragster. Eat pizza and hamburgers.

Although the park is geared for adults and teens with drivers' licenses, there's a track for kids under 42 inches. Stays open late.

Summer Hours

Sunday – Thurs. . . . . 11 am – Midnight
Fri. and Sat. . . . . 11 am – 2 am

Winter Hours

Sun. – Thurs. . . . . Noon – 10 pm
Fri. – Sat. . . . . Noon – Midnight

Cost

Top Eliminator Dragsters $12/3runs
Turbo Racers . . . . $6.50/5 minutes
Grand Prix . . $3.25/1st lap & $2.25 additional

Directions

From I-75 N, exit #271 and go east on Chastain Rd. Then right on Busbee Dr. and right again at the next light.

Amusement Parks, *Attractions And More*

PAINTBALL PLAYING FIELDS

Arkenstone Paintball Games
7257 Cedarcrest Road
Acworth, 30101
770-974-2535

Retail store, clubhouse, and 10 playing fields with ravines, forts, bunkers, foxholes, and streams. Open year-round on weekends. Age limit is 12. Birthday parties for children ages 10–13.

Paintball Atlanta
700 Holcomb Bridge Road, suite 300
Roswell, 30076
770-594-0912
www.paintball-atlanta.com

Indoor air-conditioned fields. Open year-round. Eight lighted outdoor fields with bunkers, sand mounds, ravine, trees, and a speedball field. Minimum age: 11. Full-day and half-day admissions.

Amusement Parks, Attractions And More

QZAR GAMES
3750 Venture Drive
Duluth, 30096
770-497-1313

Popular with seniors, kids

Imagine yourself wandering through this awesome maze, your heart pounding as you seek out your opponent in this incredible hi-tech game of laser tag. You aim, you fire, you're fired upon.

Your family will find this an unforgettable adventure.

Anyone big enough to wear a laser pack (children ages 6 or older) can play the game. Games last approximately 20 minutes.

Laser Quest is a popular activity for birthday parties, corporate groups, clubs, churches, and scout troops. Offers team building and customized games.

Hours

Mon. – Thurs.	2 pm – 8 pm
Friday	2 pm – Midnight
Saturday	10 am – 8 pm
Sunday	10 am – 8 pm

Cost

Person/game $7.50

Directions

From I-85 N, exit #104 (Pleasant Hill Rd). Turn left onto Pleasant Hill Rd. NW. Turn left onto Venture Dr. NW.

Amusement Parks, *Attractions And More*

SAILPLANE RIDES N GEORGIA SOARING ASSOCIATION

Monroe-Walton County Airport
404-874-3666
Atlanta High

Soar like eagles—at least just once.

The Mid-Georgia Soaring Association, the oldest and largest club of its kind in the Southeast, offers flights to anyone who would like the experience.

Flights take place on most weekends, weather permitting, from the Monroe-Walton County Airport located about 35 miles east of Atlanta.

It's then your decision. Take either the 30-minute flight, a 5280-feet tow or the 20-minute flight, a 3000-foot tow. Either way, you'll have plenty to talk about back home.

If you want to learn how to fly a sailplane, join the club; they'll teach you.

Hours
Weekends, by appointment only

Cost
$75 and $100

Directions
From US 78, take the Spring St. (GA 10) exit into Monroe. Turn South onto Madison Ave. Go 1.2 miles to Towler St. Turn left towards the airport.

Amusement Parks, *Attractions And More*

SIX FLAGS OVER GEORGIA

7561 Six Flags Road S.W.
Mableton, GA 300059
770-948-9290, www.sixflags.com

Giant theme park, huge fun

Over a hundred rides. Don't think you're going to do this in a day. That's why 2-day and season passes are bargains.

Thrill-seekers beware.

The new roller coaster Georgia Scorcher whirls you through high-speed spirals and a figure eight loop up to 4Gs, standing up. Start screaming now.

Halloween is always a kick. Concerts sometimes draw big name performers; most performances come with admission.

Dog kennels, strollers, and little storage lockers available. Food in the park's expensive. Many bring their coolers for a picnic out front. The Carrot Club (restaurant), however, is always a hit with kids. Parking $8.

Hours

(Open weekends March–mid-May, Sept. & Oct.)
Memorial Day through Labor Day
Daily . . . . 10 am–closing time varies

Cost

Adults $39.99
Children up to 48 inches $19.99
Seniors/Children under 3 . . . . Free

Directions

From I-20W, exit the Six Flags exit. MARTA: Take bus #201 from Hightower station.

SKYDIVING

Skydive Monroe

770-207-9164, www.skydivemonroe.com

Here's a fun and safe way to check skydiving off your list of thrills. Certified instructors teach sound skydiving skills and stay with you the whole time. Year round, weather permitting.

Cost
Weekends $160
Weekdays $149

Directions
From Atlanta, take 85N to Hwy 316. Go 13.1 miles. Turn right on Harbins Rd. Go 3.6 miles; turn right onto Bold Springs Rd. Go 11 miles; turn right on Hwy. 11. Go 3.7 miles; turn left at airport sign. Cross tracks and turn right on Madison. Go 1/2 mile and turn left on Towler Lane.

Atlanta Skydiving Center

Cedartown Airport, 500 Airport Road
Cedartown 30125, 770-614-3483

Specializing in first-time jumpers. Your age must be at least 18 and you must weigh under 285 pounds. Call for times and prices. A day-trip from Atlanta.

Directions
Take I-20 W to Thornton Rd., exit #44. Turn right on Thornton Rd. (Hwy 278). Follow 20 minutes; cross over Hwy 101 and the RR tracks. Go 5.5 miles from tracks; turn right at airport sign. Airport Rd. forks; stay left. The center is 1/4 miles down on left.

THUNDER ROAD USA GEORGIA RACING HALL OF FAME

415 Highway 53 East
Dawsonville, GA 30534
706-216-7223
www.thunderroadusa.com

Motorsporting's Appalachian roots

Have you ever wanted to get your hands on a race car? The Hall of Fame's high-tech racing simulators let you race with the pros. Lots of hands-on exhibits.

Once your need for speed's gone, settle into the historical aspects of racing. The sport of auto racing started in Dawsonville.

Watch footage of famous races, listen to former drivers tell their stories. Plan 2 to 3 hours to see it all.

The 44,000 square-foot facility includes a full-service restaurant and sits in a park with picnic tables and bike trails.

Hours

Open early summer 2001

Directions

Located in downtown Dawsonville, 45 miles from Atlanta. Take GA-400 N exit #87, towards Buckhead/Cumming. Take GA-53.

Amusement Parks, Attractions And More

WHITE WATER ATLANTA

250 N. Cobb Parkway NE
Marietta 30062
770-424-9283
www.whitewaterpark.com

Have a splashing-good time

Take a 9-story splash.

White Water Atlanta has the tallest free-falling slides in the world. On a hot summer day in Georgia, this is the place to be.

Or you can bob around in the Atlanta Ocean (wave pool). Fun for all ages.

Swimming suits and towel are a must. Bring plenty of sun screen and maybe a picnic lunch. (Food can't come into the park, but there are picnic tables outside the front gate.) Concessions available.

Showers and lockers available. Season passes really do save.

Hours
Daily .... 10 am – closing time varies

Cost
Adults $26.99
Children ages 3 to 48 in. $16.99
Children under 2 .... Free
Seniors $10
Nightwater (after 4 pm ..... $15.99 (for all)

Directions (20 minutes from Atlanta)
From I-75, exit #265. Follow the signs. Next to American Adventures Amusement Park.

Locations:
1. 1848 House
2. Bones
3. Brasserie Le Coze
4. Buckhead Diner
5. Canoe
6. Doc Chey's Noodle House
7. Hanwoori
8. Horseradish Grill
9. Kamogawa
10. Mary Mac's Tea Room
11. Mumbo Jumbo
12. Nava
13. Oh ... Maria!
14. OK Cafe
15. Royal China
16. Swan Coach House
17. Taqueria del Sol
18. The Flying Biscuit Cafe
19. Thelma's Kitchen
20. Watershed

Chapter 6
EATING OUT IN ATLANTA

1848 House	128
Bones	129
Brasserie Le Coze	130
Buckhead Diner	131
Canoe	132
Doc Chey's Noodle House	133
Hanwoori	134
Horseradish Grill	135
Kamogawa	136
Mary Mac's Tea Room	137
Mumbo Jumbo	138
Nava	139
Oh...Maria!	140
OK Cafe	141
Royal China	142
Swan Coach House	143
Taqueria del Sol	144
The Flying Biscuit Cafe	145
Thelma's Kitchen	146
Watershed	147

Eating Out in Atlanta

1848 HOUSE

780 S. Cobb Dr.
Marietta 30060
770-428-1848

New Southern

Every tourist comes to Atlanta looking for Tara. Those who venture to the nearby suburb of Marietta will find it at this antebellum mansion turned fine-dining venue. It is a treat at brunch when you can wander about the rooms as you help yourself to the lavish buffet. And then afterwards you can stroll through the gardens. At night, chef Thomas McEachern serves updated Southern cooking. Think downhome ingredients like grits and country ham put to the service of stylish cuisine. There's still a place for old-fashioned charm in trend-happy Atlanta.

Hours

Tues. – Sat. .... 6 pm – 9:30 pm
Sunday Jazz Brunch ...... 10:30 am – 2:30 pm
Sunday (Dinner) .... 5:30 pm – 8 pm

Cost

Sunday Jazz Brunch (all-you-can-eat) . $19.95
Dinner .... $17.95 – $28.95

Directions

Exit at the Lockheed Dobbins (exit #261). Travel west 4.3 miles. Turn right at Pearl St. About 300 feet on your left is the main gate.

Eating Out in *Atlanta*

BONE'S

3130 Piedmont Road N.E.
Atlanta 30305
404-237-2663

New American

There may be multiple branches of the top national steakhouse chains (Morton's of Chicago, Ruth's Chris Steak House) but this homegrown classic still tops the charts. There are a dozen reasons for Bone's everlasting popularity: the who's who in the crowd, the amazing wine list, the dark and clubby atmosphere, the signature deep-fried grits fritters, and the salt-baked "Seabreeze" potatoes to name a few. But the real drawing card is the USDA prime steaks, served in unadorned glory on the plate and cooked exactly the way you specified.

Hours

Lunch

Mon. – Fri. . . . . 11:30 am – 2:30 pm

Dinner

Sun. – Thurs. . . . . 5:30 pm – 10:30 pm
Fri. – Sat. . . . . 5:30 pm – 11 pm

Cost

Lunch . . . . $15 – $25
Dinner . . . . $55 – $65

Directions

Follow Piedmont Rd. south from the intersection of Peachtree Rd., and look for the restaurant on the right after a quarter mile.

Eating Out in Atlanta

BRASSERIE LE COZE

3393 Peachtree Road N.E.
Atlanta 30326
404-266-1440

French

This baby brother to New York's famed Le Bernardin is the most attractive and epicurean restaurant you could ever hope to find in a mall. Spend the day shopping at Lenox Square, then finish up at this stunningly reproduced French brasserie, complete with mirrored walls, tiled floors, brass railings and waiters in long aprons. Wonderful truffled white bean soup and skate wings with brown butter are the signature dishes, but all fish dishes shine and the pastries have style and presence. Also check for daily specials, like pan-roasted monkfish. Even the patio, facing the vastness of the Lenox Square parking lot, manages romance.

Hours

Lunch

Mon. – Thurs.	11:30 am – 2:30 pm
Friday	11:30 am – 3 pm
Saturday	11:30 – 3:30 pm

Between lunch and dinner there is an abbreviated menu available in the cafe and bar area.

Dinner

Mon. – Thurs.	5:30 pm – 10 pm
Fri. – Sat.	5:30 pm – 11 pm

Cost

Lunch	$7 – $12
Dinner	$10 – $25

Directions

In Lenox Square Mall, in the heart of Buckhead.

Eating Out in Atlanta

BUCKHEAD DINER

3073 Piedmont Road
Atlanta 30305
404-262-3336

New American

You don't think of the words "diner" and glamour in one breath, unless you're at this lustrous Buckhead institution. The sleek chrome exterior rises from the street like an icon from another era and always has a line-up of sexy sports cars parked in front.

Inside, the counter-flanked open kitchen and deep booths wittily reference the design of Pullman-car diners. And yet the carpets, fabrics and wall treatments all belong to the world of fine dining. You can't miss the signature house-made potato chips with melted Maytag blue cheese. After that you have your choice of veal meatloaf with celery mashed potatoes, upscale fish presentations, and even foot-long hot dogs.

The white chocolate banana cream pie—a local legend—ends the meal on a memorable note.

Hours

Mon. – Sat. . . . . 11 am – Midnight
Sunday . . . . 10 am – 10 pm

Cost

Lunch . . . . $10 – $17
Dinner . . . . $16 – $23

Directions

Follow Piedmont Rd. south from the intersection of Peachtree Rd., and look for the restaurant on the left after half a mile.

Eating Out in Atlanta

CANOE

4199 Paces Ferry Road
Vinings 30339 770-432-2663

New American

The Chattahoochee River wends its way so discreetly alongside Atlanta that it would be easy to miss it entirely. This stylish, beautifully situated restaurant is the best of the few local establishments to take advantage of the 'Hooch's natural charms. Set on the west bank of the river in the upscale community of Vinings, Canoe offers contemporary fare, a fine wine program, a hot bar scene at night, and any number of perfectly placed tables and booths set along custom-designed wrought-iron railings.

Everything is made in-house, from the cornucopia of offerings in the memorable bread basket to the tortillas served with Mexican eggs at brunch. Speaking of brunch, make sure to reserve early to get a table on the patio, and don't miss the sticky buns.

Hours

(Lunch) Mon. – Fri. ..... 11:30 am – 2:30 pm
(Brunch) Sunday .... 10:30 am – 2:30 pm
(Dinner) Mon. – Thurs ..... 5:30 pm – 10 pm
(Dinner) Fri. and Sat. ...... 5:30 pm – 11 pm
(Dinner) Sunday .... 5:30 pm – 9:30 pm

Cost

Lunch .... $7 – $14
Sunday Brunch .... $8 – $16
Dinner .... $17 – $24

Directions

Follow West Paces Ferry Rd. from Buckhead west under I-75, and veer right onto Paces Ferry Rd. Follow across the river. Look for Canoe on the right.

Eating Out in Atlanta

DOC CHEY'S NOODLE HOUSE

1424 N. Highland Aveue N.E.
Atlanta 30309 404-888-0777

Asian

These two noodle houses in northeast Atlanta—one near the Emory University campus and the other in the fun shopping district of Morniningside/Virginia Highland—offer satisfyin)g, healthy pan-Asian noodles and more at low prices. For $5 or $6 you can feast on stir-fried Thai noodles with spicy basil sauce, Japanese yakisoba, Vietnamese rice noodle bowls with salad or delicious soups made with coconut curry or miso. Add good appetizers and a beer/wine list, and you get a fine meal for a budget prices. None of the food is quite as good as it would be in a more authentic restaurant, but considering the convenience and the prices, we're not complaining.

Hours

Monday .... 5 pm – 10 pm
Tues. – Thurs. & Sun. ..... 11:30 am – 10 pm
Fri. – Sun. .... 11:30 am – 11pm

Cost

$6 – $8

Directions

Follow Ponce de Leon Ave. west from Midtown. Turn left on N. Highland, and look for the restaurant on the left at the intersection of University.

Other location:
1556N. Decatur Road N.E.
Atlanta 404-378-8188

Follow Ponce de Leon Ave. west from Midtown. Turn left on Lullwater, then right on N. Decatur. Look for the restaurant immediately on the left.

Eating Out in Atlanta

HANWOORI

4251 N. Peachtree Road
Atlanta 30341
770-458-9191

Korean

Atlanta is home to a large and vibrant Korean community that offers a variety of dining options. A good start is at this spacious and attractive spot where the menus are well translated and the grand space a pleasant place to spend two hours. Korean barbecue is the order of the day. Order marinated beef bulgogi, beef short ribs and assorted other goodies, and the waitress will show you how to cook them at your tabletop and then wrap up the sizzling morsels with rice, pickled vegetables and sauce in lettuce leaves —like healthy far-Eastern tacos. Don't worry about the smoke: There's an individual exhaust hood over each and every table. And though Korean food is famously spicy, you can order mild dishes easily.

Hours

Mon. – Sun. . . . . 11 am – 11 pm

Cost

Lunch . . . . $6 – $9
Dinner . . . . $15 – $33

Directions

Take I-285 west to exit #30, (N. Peachtree Rd). Turn left onto N. Peachtree Rd. and follow it under the highway. The restaurant is on the left.

Eating Out *in Atlanta*

HORSERADISH GRILL

4320 Powers Ferry Road N.W.
Atlanta 30342   404-255-7277

New Southern

So many restaurants in Atlanta try to doll up the simple pleasures of the Southern table in bistro finery, but none do it as well as this high-energy contemporary eatery in a converted horse barn on the edge of Chastain Park.

Dishes such as grilled pork chops with sweet potato puree, roasted Georgia trout, and North Carolina pork barbecue over a corn cake manage to be down-home, simple, and elegant all at once. The wine list is carefully thought out to match the food, and the service has the brisk graciousness you'd expect from a restaurant that so neatly captures the spirit of Atlanta. The oatmeal spice cake is not to be missed.

Hours

Lunch
Mon. – Fri. . . . . 11:30 am – 2:30 pm

Dinner
Mon. – Thurs. . . . . 5:30 pm – 10 pm
Fri. – Sat. . . . . 5 pm – 11 pm
Sunday . . . . 5 pm – 9 pm

Brunch
Sunday . . . . 11 am – 2:30 pm

Cost

Lunch/Sunday brunch . . . . $7 – $14
Dinner . . . . $17 – $28

Directions

Alongside Chastain Park. Follow Powers Ferry Rd. from Roswell Rd., and look for the restaurant on the left.

Eating Out in Atlanta

KAMOGAWA

3300 Peachtree Road N.E.
Atlanta 30305
404-841-0314

Japanese

The Grand Hyatt seems an unlikely place to find a formal Japanese restaurant, But it makes sense if you know this granite tower standing tall on a Buckhead street corner used to be known as the Japanese-owned Nikko Hotel.

Walk through the hanging noren curtain to a mood of hushed serenity. The surroundings, enhanced by polished river stones and a burbling stream, are lovely. There is a communal dining area with a sushi bar at one end. Yet parties of 4 or more will want to reserve one of the Japanese-style tatami-mat rooms, where waitresses in full kimono serve you as they kneel beside the table. Start with a superlative sashimi platter and then move on to one of the one-pot dishes like shabu shabu or sukiyaki.

Hours

Lunch
Mon. – Fri. .... 11:30 am – 2 pm
Dinner
Mon. – Sun. .... 6 pm – 10 pm

Cost

Lunch .... $7.50 – $19.50
Dinner .... $10 – $40

Directions

In the Grand Hyatt on the corner of Piedmont Rd. and Peachtree Rd. in Buckhead.

Eating Out   *in Atlanta*

MARY MAC'S TEA ROOM

224 Ponce de Leon Aveue
Atlanta 30308
404-876-1800

Southern

This Southern tea room has been around as long as most present-day Atlantans can remember. The prices are low and the warren of old-fashioned rooms are crammed with tables. Look for all the Southern favorites, including fried chicken and the full range of vegetable side dishes. But also look for such outdated traditions as collard greens served with a cup of "potlikker," the salty cooking liquid, on the side. You crumble your cornbread into it and spoon it up. And if you want a glass of buttermilk, no problem. Mary Mac's is convenient to the Moorish-style Fox Theatre, the city's premium venue for musical theater.

Hours

Mon. – Sat. . . . . 11 am – 3 pm
Sunday . . . . 11 am – 8:30 pm

Cost

Lunch . . . . $7 – $15
Dinner . . . . $8 – $20

Directions

Follow Ponce de Leon Ave. west from Midtown and look for Mary Mac's on the left.

Eating Out in Atlanta

MUMBO JUMBO

89 Park Place N.E.
Atlanta 30303
404-523-0330

New American

There are a zillion choices for casual dining in downtown Atlanta. You can see the sights and happily ensconce yourself in in a food court or a cafeteria afterwards. But if you want to sit down in a comtemporary atmosphere and sample some cuisine that has style and personality, there's only Mumbo Jumbo. This former nightclub has a huge bar and lounge area and a hip, noisy restaurant in the back. Choices at lunchtime include a salad with green beans and smoked chicken, handmade pasta, and the now-famous lunch combo of a half truffled chicken salad sandwich with a bowl of Mumbo gumbo. At night, it's a great place to linger over drinks and fried calamari with jalapenos in the lounge and, if a convention isn't in town, to have an elegant dinner.

Hours

Lunch
Mon. – Fri. . . . . 11:30 am – 2:30 pm

Dinner
Mon. – Sun. . . . . 5:30 pm – 11 pm

Cost

Lunch . . . . $8 – $15
Dinner . . . . $16 – $30

Directions

On the small street to the right of Woodruff Park in the heart of downtown.

Eating Out in Atlanta

NAVA

3060 Peachtree Road N.W.
Atlanta 30305
404-240-1984

Southern

Atlanta's splashiest Southwestern restaurant keeps locals and tourists happy with the astonishing vibrancy of the decor and the cuisine, and the great spirit of fun chef Kevin Rathbun brings to the menu. The three-tiered dining room is a swirl of color and movement, with Navajo carpets and Kokopelli dancer figurines setting the sense of place. Have one of the amazing house margaritas and nibble on a basket of blue corn sticks. Then move on to mussels in red chile broth and seared tuna, and don't miss the game that is often on special. The banana quesadillas, with wrappers made solely of dried bananas, have legions of fans.

Hours

Lunch
Mon. – Fri. . . . . 11:30 am – 2:30 pm

Dinner
Mon. – Thurs. . . . . 5:30 pm – 11 pm
Friday . . . . 5:30 pm – Midnight
Saturday . . . . 5 pm – Midnight
Sunday . . . . 5:30 pm – 10 pm

Cost

Lunch . . . . $4.95 – $15.95
Dinner . . . . $14.50 – $27.95

Directions

On the corner of Peachtree Rd. and West Paces Ferry Rd. in central Buckhead.

Eating Out in Atlanta

OH... MARIA!

3167 Peachtree Road
Atlanta 30305
404-261-2032

Mexican

Like so many of Atlanta's better restaurants, Oh...Maria! inhabits a nondescript strip shopping center. But the inside of this Mexican restaurant is a fantastic sight. Candles—some as tall as 4 feet—flicker from the floors and the walls. A glass wall separating the bar from the dining room is lined with shelves of gorgeous tequila bottles. Mexican crafts and artwork fill every nook. The menu offers contemporary Mexican cuisine—chicken with velvety mole sauces, pan-seared snapper, and salads made with cactus paddles and jicama. But you may be happiest ordering the fantastic appetizers made from fresh corn masa and trying one of those tequilas. For dessert, don't miss the crepes served with the goat's-milk caramel called cajeta.

Hours

Dinner

Mon.–Thurs. .... 5:30 pm – 11 pm
Friday .... 5:30 pm – Midnight

Weekends

Saturday .... 1 pm – Midnight
Sunday (Brunch/Dinner) ...... 1 pm – 10 pm

Cost

Under $20

Directions

On the corner of Peachtree Rd. and Grandview Rd. in central Buckhead.

Eating Out in Atlanta

OK CAFE

1284 W. Paces Ferry Road N.W.
Atlanta 30327
404-233-2888

American

Start off a morning in Buckhead with breakfast at this local favorite. You will find it packed with the Atlanta power elite sitting side by side with construction workers, and everyone enjoying heaping platters of Southern breakfast—eggs, grits, ham and biscuits. Kids will particularly sit within sight of the money tree festooned with dollar bills. The restaurant is open 24 hours a day, and Atlantans love the inventive vegetables, such as baked sweet potatoes with pecans.

Hours

Sun. – Thurs. . . . . 7 am – 11 pm
Fri. – Sat. . . . . open 24 hours

Cost

$7 – $13

Directions

On the corner of West Paces Ferry Rd. and Northside Dr. in western Buckhead, alongside I-75.

Eating Out in Atlanta

ROYAL CHINA

3295 Chamblee Dunwoody Road
Chamblee 30341
770-216-9933

Chinese

Atlanta's best ethnic dining area is the stretch of Buford Highway that passes between the northern suburbs of Chamblee and Doraville. There are many fine eating adventures to be had, not the least of which is Royal China's excellent dim sum. This Cantonese-style feast of tea pastries passes by your table on rolling carts, so even if you don't know the names of the various dumplings, fritters, and nibbles, you can just point. The restaurant also serves Cantonese seafood day and night. But the lavish dim sum is the reason you want to go.

Hours

Mon. – Sun. . . . . 11 am – 10:30 pm

Cost

Entrees start at $7.50

Directions

Follow Buford Highway north from Buckhead; turn left on Chamblee Dunwoody Rd. and look for the restaurant on the right.

Eating Out   *in Atlanta*

SWAN COACH HOUSE

3130 Slaton Dr.
Atlanta 30325
404-261-0636

Southern

After a visit to the Atlanta History Center and the Swan House, the historic mansion that is part of the complex, you'll be filled with visions of magnolias and dogwoods and the gracious ways of old Atlanta. Should you want to linger in the old South just a little longer, visit this tearoom set in the coach house of the grand property. It is strictly a ladies-who-lunch kind of place, where gloves and bonnets are not out of place. Specialties include chicken salad served with a side of frozen fruit salad and cheese straws. Not a favorite among guys, but ladies daintily sip this place up.

Hours

Mon. – Sat. .... 11:30 am – 2:30 pm

Cost

$7.50 – $10.50

Directions

Follow Peachtree Rd. north from Midtown. Turn left on West Paces Ferry Rd. and then left on Slaton Dr. just beyond the Atlanta History Center.

Eating Out in Atlanta

TAQUERIA DEL SOL
1200 Howell Mill Road N.W. #B
Atlanta 30318
404-352-5811

Mexican/Southern

Located amidst the antique stores and stylish industrial rehabs in the Westside development, this new-age taqueria routinely has a line snaking out the door at lunch and at dinner. And with good reason! The $1.95 tacos, ranging from Memphis BBQ with coleslaw to fried fish with jalapeno tartar sauce, are superb. Order a couple of tacos and a side dish such as Mexican rice, spicy turnip greens, or creamy poblano soup, and you have a gourmet meal in a plastic basket. The chips with freshly made salsa and cheese dip are also fine, and the Westside margaritas taste awfully good alongside.

For a more substantial meal, don't miss the daily specials.

Hours
Lunch
Mon. – Fri. .... 11 am – 2 pm
Saturday .... Noon – 3 pm
Dinner
Tues. – Thurs. .... 5:30 pm – 9 pm
Fri. – Sat. .... 5:30 pm – 10 pm

Cost
$1.65 – $7.95

Directions
Follow Marietta St. north from downtown. Veer left onto Howell Mill Rd. Look for the restaurant on the left, after the intersection of 14th Ave.

Eating Out in Atlanta

THE FLYING BISCUIT CAFE

1655 McLendon Aveue
Atlanta 30307
404-687-8888

Eclectic American

Weekend brunches are the big draw to this Candler Park success story. The brunches attract crowds who are happy to mill around the neighborhood for an hour, coffee cups in hand, waiting for a table and exploring the funky shops.

The enormous biscuits with apple butter are just for starters. Eggs, homemade turkey sausage, and black bean "love cakes" manage to bridge the worlds of health food and sophisticated dining. The restaurant also serves lunch and dinner, and choices include healthy burritos, fresh fish specials, and meatloaf with the well-seasoned mashed potatoes called "pudge." The colorful dining rooms with handpainted murals have the spirit of latter-day hippie chic. The bakery next door sells coffee drinks and a wide variety of breakfast pastries to go.

Hours

Sun. – Thurs. . . . . 8:30 am – 10 pm
Fri. – Sat. . . . . 8:30 am – 10:30 pm

Cost

Lunch . . . . $2.95 – $8.50
Dinner . . . . $6.95 – $12.95

Directions

Follow Ponce de Leon Ave. west from Midtown, turn right on Moreland Ave., then left onto McLendon. The restaurant is on the right.

Eating Out *in Atlanta*

THELMA'S KITCHEN
768 Marietta Street
Atlanta 30316
404-688-5855

Southern

Thelma Grundy's beloved downtown "meat and two" was one of the victims of progress when Atlanta put a new face on downtown before the Olympics.

Thelma's customers were overjoyed when she reopened further up the street and once again began serving the soul food for which she is famous. There's nothing fancy in the looks or on the menu of this downhome cafeteria—just great fried chicken, collards, black-eyed peas, cornbread, fresh pies and tea as sweet as sweet can be. Executives from Coca-Cola and CNN often show up at Thelma's. Don't be surprised if you see Ted Turner at the next table.

Hours
Mon. – Fri. . . . . 7:30 am – 4:30 pm
Saturaday . . . . 7:30 am – 3 pm

Cost
$6.06 – $9.25

Directions

Follow Marietta Street north from Five Points; Thelma's will be on the left, near the Coca-Cola complex.

Eating Out   *in Atlanta*

WATERSHED

406 W. Ponce de Leon Avenue
Decatur 30030
404-378-4900

Southern cuisine with an Italian flair

This quirky Decatur spot, partially owned by Emily Saliers of the Indigo Girls, started life as a carry-out market, gift shop, and wine bar with only a few sandwiches and such on the menu. With the spread of the fame, the restaurant seating was increased and the menu expanded to make Watershed one the best and most original in the metro area. The food is expensive, given the casual setting but it is often spectacular. Spaghetti with Georgia white shrimp and garlic, bruschetta with wild mushrooms, amazing nightly soups, the "Very Good Chocolate Cake," and the pecan tart are the headliners. But everyone in Atlanta knows that chef Scott Peacock makes his famous fried chicken dinner with real Southern biscuits on Tuesdays only, and it's an early sellout. Is there better fried chicken on the planet?

Hours
Mon. – Sat. .... 11 am – 10 pm

Cost
$12 – $25

Directions
Follow Ponce de Leon toward downtown Decatur from Atlanta. After it becomes West Ponce de Leon, look for Watershed on the right.

Locations
1. Four Season Hotel
2. Grand Hyatt Atlanta
3. Ritz-Carlton Atlanta
4. Ritz-Carlton Buckhead
5. Swissotel Atlanta
6. Ansley Inn
7. Beverly Hills Manor
8. Gaslight Inn
9. Heartfield Manor
10. King-Keith House
11. Sugar Magnolia Bed & Breakfast
12. Shellmont Bed & Breakfast
13. Virginia Highland Inn
14. Historic days Inn
15. Holiday Inn Midtown North
16. Sleep Inn/Mainstay Suites
17. Summerfield Suites
18. Georgian Terrace
19. Callaway Gardens
20. Chateau Elan Winery & Resort
21. Lake Lanier Resort

Chapter 7
WHERE TO STAY

Atlanta Luxury Hotels

    Four Seasons Hotel 152

    Grand Hyatt Atlanta 152

    Ritz-Carlton Atlanta 153

    Ritz-Carlton Buckhead 153

    Swissotel Atlanta 153

Bed & Breakfast Inns

    Ansley Inn 154

    Beverly Hills Inn 154

    Gaslight Inn 155

    Heartfield Manor 155

    King-Keith House 156

    Sugar Magnolia Bed & Breakfast 156

    Shellmont Bed & Breakfast 157

    Virgina Highland Inn 157

Best Value Hotels

    Historic Days Inn 158

    Holiday Inn Midtown North 158

    Sleep Inn/Mainstay Suites 159

    Summerfield Suites 159

Historic Hotels

    Georgian Terrace 160

Resorts

    Callaway Gardens 160

    Chateau Elan Winery & Resort 161

    Lake Lanier Resort 161

Where to Stay?

ATLANTA LUXURY HOTELS
Four Seasons Hotel

75 14th St. N.E.
Atlanta 30309
404-881-9898

This 50-story, red granite, black-glass building with a stunning facade is located in Midtown near the Woodruff Arts Center—Atlanta's hub for the arts.

Indoor pool, health club, 24-hour room service, full-service restaurant, cable TV, and much more. World-class status, you'll find woolen blankets, down pillows, and terry cloth bathrobes. Children under 16 stay free in parents' room. Pets under 25 pounds allowed. MARTA one block away. (Between Peachtree St. and West Peachtree St.)

Average rates
$290 – $550 (for suites)

Grand Hyatt Atlanta

3300 Peachtree Road N.E.
Atlanta 30305
404-365-8100

The stately, 25-story hotel's exterior resembles a bank. But inside the posh lobby features a lush Japanese garden complete with waterfalls. Located in Buckhead, minutes from Lenox Square. Rooms with dark colors and rich woods. Sundeck, fitness center, and sushi bar. Pets under 25 pounds allowed. Children stay free in parents' room. Fax machines and fog-free mirrors. (At Piedmont Rd.)

Average rates
$119 – $395

Where to Stay?

Ritz-Carlton Atlanta

181 Peachtree St. N.E.
Atlanta 30303, 404-659-0400

Serious luxury. Atlanta's downtown 25-story highrise is close to many downtown attractions and sports venues. Marble tubs, down pillows, terry cloth robes, cordless phones. A technology butler is on staff. (On Peachtree and Ellis Sts. MARTA's Peachtree station is only 1 block away.)

Average rates
$225 – $325

Ritz-Carlton Buckhead

3434 Peachtree Road N.E.
Atlanta 30326, 404-237-2700

The undramatic exterior is no indication of this hotel's ultimate luxury. Marble-topped desks, goose-down pillows, high-speed internet access. Houses the city's most popular restaurant—the Buckhead Diner. Best Sunday brunch. And one of the Southeast's finest collections of early 18th-century paintings. (Across from Lenox Square.)

Average rates
$225 – $1500 (for a suite with a baby grand piano)

Swissotel Atlanta

3391 Peachtree Road N.e.
Atlanta 30326, 404-365-0065

Rooms—elegant, spacious with a European decor. Valet service, a health and massage center, 24-hour fitness club, television speakers in bathroom. Within walking distance of Lenox Square. Located in the heart of Atlanta's business and shopping district. (Between Lenox and Piedmont Roads.)

Average rates
$180 – $450

Where to Stay?

BED & BREAKFAST INNS

Ansley Inn
253 15th Street
Atlanta 30309
404-872-9000

Cozy inn, cozy upscale neighborhood. You won't want to leave. Delightful old English Tudor mansion with 22 suites. Many have fireplaces. Clothing magnate George Muse built the house in 1907.

Excellent location for attending performances at the Fox Theatre. Many chic restaurants in the vicinity.(Peachtree St. and 15th Sts.)

Average rates
$109 – $189

Beverly Hills Inn
65 Sheridan Drive N.E.
Atlanta 30305
404-233-8520

Only minutes away from Lenox Squae and Phipps Plaza, this 1929 four-story inn makes you feel like you're in Europe. Once an upscale apartment building, the inn's rooms come with kitchens, balconies, cable television, and data ports. Recommended as one of the most romantic places to stay. Has been featured in many popular vacation magazines. Eat breakfast on the patio. Atlanta's first bed and breakfast inn.

Average rates
$125 per night

Where  *to Stay?*

Gaslight Inn

1001 Saint Charles Avenue N.E.
Atlanta 30306
404-875-1001

You've seen the inn featured on television; it's that nice. World-class quality. Professionally decorated by a prestigious design firm. Named for the flickering gaslight fixtures used to light the inn. A screened porch, cable TV, books, baby grand piano, and a large selection of CDs make the stay enjoyable. Have breakfast in the formal dining room, in the flower garden, or on the front porch. Wicker chairs and swing. (East of downtown in the Virginia-Highlands.)

Average rate
$95 – $195

Heartfield Manor

182 Elizabeth Street
Atlanta 30307
404-523-8633

Located in charming Inman Park, the inn's three rooms and three suites are decorated with period furnishing. Children welcome. The house backs up to a park with a playground. Mornings begin with fresh fruit and bagels. Located only 7 blocks from restaurants and theaters. Only 2 1/2 blocks from MARTA.

Average rates
Rooms $65 - $70
Suites $75 - $95

Where to Stay?

King-Keith House

889 Edgewood Avenue
Atlanta 30307
404-688-7330 or 800-728-3879

Features of this old home include a wraparound porch with an attached gazebo and lace-work arches. Considered the oldest home in Inman Park. Once the residents of a hardware magnate George King. Located two miles from downtown and within two blocks of MARTA. The innkeepers will provide transportation to nearby events and attractions.

Five guest rooms. Enjoy private baths, antiques, and a full breakfast. Rooms come with 12-foot ceilings and fireplaces.

Average rates
$95-$175

Sugar Magnolia Bed & Breakfast

804 Edgewood Avenue N.E.
Atlanta 30307
404-222--0226

A late 19th-century Queen Anne Victorian home located in historic Inman Park. House has wraparound porch, elegant sitting rooms, and a grand staircase. Enjoy cozy large rooms, fireplaces, private baths, and hardwood floors. Breakfast comes to your room. Ask for the Royal Suite. Comes with 2 balconies, an aristocrat's bed, and a sunken bath. A house with a lot of charm and character.

Outside, gardens have a waterfall. Afternoon tea served. A great price value.

Average rates
$85 – $125

Where to Stay?

Shellmont Bed & Breakfast

821 Piedmont Avenue N.E.
Atlanta 30308
404-872-9290

An 1891 Victorian home in Midtown. Sits behind large pine trees. Stained-glass windows, beautiful antique furniture, and plenty of charm. Private baths, bathrobes, and queen-size beds. Some rooms with kitchenettes, jacuzzis, and balconies. Complimentary breakfasts, desserts, fresh fruits, and chocolates. Only a few minutes from the Woodruff Arts Center. (From I-75/85 N., take International Blvd. exit. Turn left at 2nd light, Ellis St., turn right at next traffic light, Piedmont Ave. Go north 1 1/4 miles.)

Average rates
$120 – $150

Virginia Highland Inn

630 Orme Circle
Atlanta 30306
404-892-2735 or 877-870-4489
www.virginiahighlanbb.com
www.mindspring.com/~thevahighlandbandb

The innkeeper enjoys cooking wonderful breakfasts for her guests. Eat either in the kitchen or formal dining room. Guests love the 1920s feel to the two bungalow suites and the innkeeper's prized garden. Rooms come with private entrances, sitting proches, and baths.

Averge rates
$125 per night

Where to Stay?

BEST VALUE HOTELS

Historic Days Inn

683 Peachtree Street N.E.
Atlanta 30308
404-874-9200

Built in 1924, the 12-story building once served as a bachelor apartment complex. It was remodeled in 1996 and now has 139 rooms with Southern antiques and mahogany beams.

In Midtown, across from the Fox Theater, the hotel's centrally located to downtown and many attractions. (Between Ponce de Leon Avenue and 3rd Street.)

Average rates
$59 – $269

Holiday Inn Midtown North

1810 Howell Mill Road N.W.
Atlanta 30318
404-351-3831

Hotel with 201 guest rooms. On the boundary of Midtown on an overlooked industrial street now blooming with loft apartments. Conveniently located. Children under 19 stay free with their parents. The Green Derby Restaurant offers cheap eats with kids under 12 eating free with paying parents.

You'll find an outdoor pool, fitness center, cable TV, microwave ovens, and refrigerators. Currently, the hotel is renovating its rooms and exterior. (Three miles north of downtown. From I-75, exit 252B.)

Average rates
$79.99 – $99

Where  **to Stay?**

Sleep Inn/Mainstay Suites

800 Sidney Marcus Boulevard
Atlanta 30324
404-949-4000

New hotels with easy highway access make getting to destinations a breeze. Located a short distance from Buckhead with a complimentary bus that takes you there. One and two bedroom suites with fully equipped kitchens. Complimentary Continental breakfast, fitness center, outdoor pool, 24-hour business center, and laundry service.

Children 18 and under stay free with their parents. MARTA Lindbergh station only a block away. (From I-85 N, exit onto Highway 86, Buford Highway. Take the service road 2 miles to the 1st light, turn left under the freeway onto Sidney Marcus.)

Average rates
$69 – $119

Summerfield Suites

505 Pharr Street
Atlanta 30305
404-262-7880

Great Buckhead location. Feels homey. Offers large spacious 2 bedroom, 2 bath suites with kitchens for family travelers. And a 1 bedroom suite for business travelers. Free breakfast buffet. Exercise room and outdoor pool with whirlpool. High-speed internet access, large desks, and speaker phones. (Six miles from downtown, Take I-85 N to Buford Hwy. Exit at Piedmont Rd. N and follow to Pharr Rd. Turn left.)

Average rates
$99 – $149

Where to Stay?

HISTORIC HOTELS
Georgian Terrace
659 Peachtree Street
Atlanta 30308
404-897-1991

The old Atlanta gem with an interesting history. *Gone With The Wind*'s actors, Vivien Leigh and Clark Gable, stayed while making the movie. The premiere party took place in the lobby.

Fully restored in 1997, the hotel looks much like it did originally, with new modern amenities.

You'll enjoy a rooftop pool, internet connections, and a health club.

Located within a short drive of many attractions. (Peachtree Street and Ponce de Leon.)

Average rates
$109 – $1000

RESORTS
Callaway Gardens
Highway 27
Pine Mountain 31822
706-663-2281

A 2500-acre horticulture delight—manicured and in a natural way. Resort includes a fishing lake, tennis courts, hiking, biking, a gun club, lakeside beaches, and championship golf courses. Butterfly Center and the largest conservatory. Visit the Discover Center. Skeet shooting and fly fishing. Great get-away or resort vacation. Accommodations on site. (Take I-85 S. to I-185, then to Highway 27.)

Average rates
$119 per night

Where  **to Stay?**

Chateau Elan Winery & Resort

100 Rue Charlemagne
Braselton 30517
678-425-6000

The winery flourished into a world-class, 4-star resort with seven restaurants, four great golf courses, a tennis center, a spa, tennis center, and an equestrian show center. Stay at the 277-room inn. Rooms come with oversized tubs, separate showers, and country French furnishings. The spa's 14 rooms come with uniquely decorated rooms including Art Deco, Western, Oriental, Gatsby, and Greek. No pets. (Take I-85 N. Turn left on Highway 211.)

Average rates
$109 – $189

Lake Lanier Resort

6950 Holiday Road
Buford 30518
770-932-7255

A scenic, 1200-acre lakefront resort. The biggest attractions are the beaches and water park. Visitors can rent houseboats, sailboats, skiboats. Landlovers can hike the trails, rent bikes, and ride horseback along the shores. Two championship golf courses. Great day trip or stay in one of the two resort hotels, a waterfront rental house, or at the campground. (From I-85 N., exit #113, I-985. Then exit GA-20.)

Average rates
Call for hotels' special rates

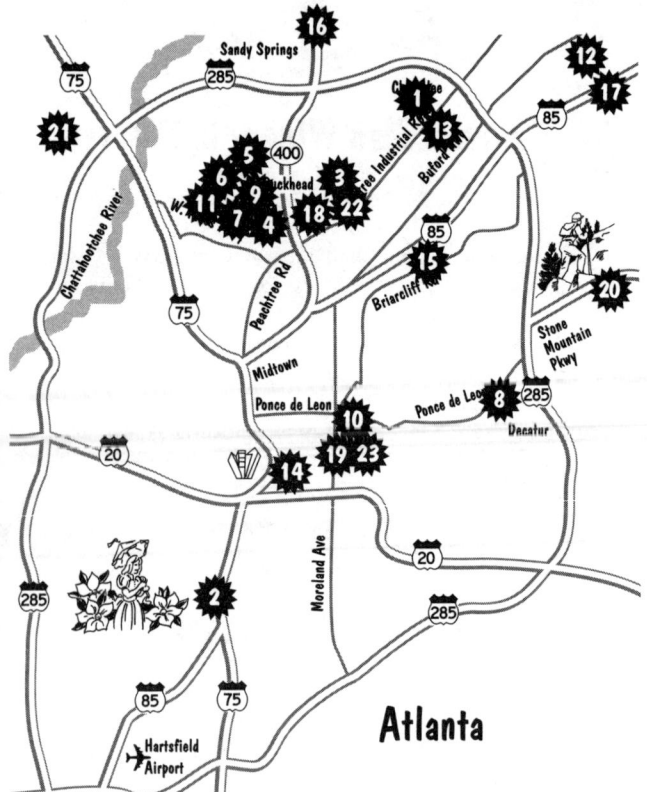

Locations:
Antique Shops
1. Chamblee's Antique Row
2. Lakewood Antiques Market

Art Galleries
3. Connell Gallery
4. Frabel Studio and Gallery
5. Jackson Fine Art
6. The Lowe Gallery
7. Trinity Gallery Buckhead
8. By Hand South
9. Signature Shop and Gallery
10. Van Gogh
11. Vermilion Gallery

Flea Markets
12. A Flea An'tique
13. Buford Highway Flea Market

Food Markets
14. Sweet Auburn Curb Market
15. Whole Foods Market

Outlet Stores
16. North Georgia Premium Outlets
17. Tanger Outlet Center

Unique Places To Shop
18. Lenox Square & Phipps Plaza
19. Little Five Points
20. Stone Mountain Village

Unique Shops
21. Brumby Chair Company
22. Build-A-Bear Workshop
23. Junkman's Daughter

Chapter 8
UNIQUE PLACES TO SHOP

Antique Shops
- Chamblee's Antique Row 162
- Lakewood Antiques Market 162

Art Galleries - Atlanta's best fine art galleries
- Connell Gallery 163
- Frabel Studio and Gallery 163
- Jackson Fine Art.......................... 163
- The Lowe Gallery 163
- Trinity Gallery Buckhead 163

Art Galleries - Atlanta's best affordable art galleries
- By Hand South 164
- Signature Shop and Gallery 164
- Van Gogh 164
- Vermilion Gallery 164

Flea Markets
- A Flea An'tique 165
- Buford Highway Flea Market 165

Food Markets
- Sweet Auburn Curb Market 166
- Whole Foods Market 166

Outlet Stores
- North Georgia Premium Outlets 167
- Tanger Outlet Center 167

Unique Places To Shop
- Lenox Square & Phipps Plaza 168
- Little Five Points 168
- Stone Mountain Village 168

Unique Shops
- Brumby Chair Company 169
- Build-A-Bear Workshop.................. 169
- Junkman's Daughter...................... 169

Unique Places  *to Shop*

ANTIQUE SHOPS

Chamblee's Antique Row
3550 Broad Street
Chamblee 30341
770-458-6316

Even the buildings are antiques. Many dealers locate in old mid-1800 houses, churches, and stores. About twenty buildings piled high with antiques— the South's largest antique area. Over 200 dealers. Take I-85 to I-285 going west. Exit Peachtree Industrial Blvd. and follow 1.5 miles to Broad St. Go left. MARTA: Chamblee station.

Mon. – Sat. . . . . 10 am – 5:30 pm
Sunday . . . . 1 pm – 5:30 pm

Lakewood Antiques Market
2000 Lakewood Avenue S.W.
Atlanta 30315
404-622-4488

You never know what you'll find; that's the fun. Named one of America's top five antique shows. Held the 2nd Saturday of every month at the Lakewood Fairgrounds. Thursday is "Early Buyer Day." Spaces for 1500 dealers. Find rare antiques and architectural treasures. I-75 S., exit #243. Go east on 166.

Thurs., Fri., & Sat. . . . . 9 am – 6 pm
Sunday . . . . 10 am – 5 pm

Unique Places to Shop

ART GALLERIES
Atlanta's best fine art galleries

Connell Gallery
333 Buckhead Avenue,
Atlanta 30305, 404-261-1712
Atlanta's finest in studio crafts: glass, fiber,
furniture, jewelry, clay, and more.

Frabel Studio and Gallery
695 Antone Street N.W.,
Atlanta 30318, 404-351-9794
World-renowned studio for flame-worked crystal.
Watch artists at work. Stunning works
displayed in gallery.

Jackson Fine Art
3115 East Shadowlawn Avenue,
Atlanta 30305, 404-233-3739
Atlanta's top gallery. Specializing in 20th-century
and contemporary works. Photography.

The Lowe Gallery
75 Bennett Street, Space A-2
Atlanta 30309, 404-352-8114
Atlanta's leader in internationally renowned
contemporary artists. Sixty artists
represented.

Trinity Gallery Buckhead
315 East Paces Ferry Road
Atlanta 30305, 404-237-0370
Atlanta's leading fine art store. Emerging and
well-known artists.

Unique Places to Shop

ART GALLERIES
Atlanta's best affordable art galleries

By Hand South
112 East Ponce de Leon Avenue
Decatur 30030
404-378-0118
Beautiful contemporary American crafts; pottery, fine art glass, jewelry, and other handmade objects.

Signature Shop and Gallery
3267 Roswell Road N.W.
Atlanta 30305
404-237-4426
Wonderfully handcrafted dinnerware, art glass, jewelry, and hand-bound books. Contemporary crafts.

Van Gogh
1651 McLendon Avenue N.E.
Atlanta 30307
404-370-1003
Nothing over $500. Local handicrafts. Pottery, candles, paintings, wood cravings, and more.

Vermilion Gallery
1244 W. Paces Ferry Road
Atlanta 30327
404-869-9845
Here's an excellent selection of comtemporary crafts, paintings (regional artists), fine crafts, hand-blown glass.

Unique Places  *to Shop*

FLEA MARKETS

A Flea An'tique
4300 Highway 20 N.E.
Buford 30518
770-932-6833

An upscale flea market? Only in downtown Buford. You'll find antiques, 50s-style furniture, collectors' items, and decorator items. Tucked away in the mountains, 30 miles from Atlanta. Take I-85 N to I-985. Turn off on the 1st exit and go left 2 miles.

Daily . . . . 10 am – 7 pm

Buford Highway Flea Market
5000 Buford Highway
Chamblee 30341
770-452-7140

You say it, they've got it. Plenty of unusual finds at this typical flea market. Never the same from week to week. That's half the fun. Open Fridays, Saturdays, and Sundays. From I-85 N, exit Chamblee/Tucker Rd. and go left on Chamblee Rd. Then right on Buford Highway. The market is 1/2 block down on the left.

Fri. & Sat. 11 am – 9 pm
Sunday . . . . 11 – 8 pm

Unique Places to Shop

FOOD MARKETS

Sweet Auburn Curb Market
209 Edgewood Avenue S.W.
Atlanta 30303
404-659-1665

Soul food. Southern cooking. Sample Atlanta's rich culture at this African-American food market. Popular with tourists visiting the Martin Luther King historical sites and museums. Indoor/outdoor seating. African-American grocery store. Produce, meats, bakery, and more. At the corner of Edgewood Avenue and Butler Street.

Mon.–Thurs. . . . . 8 am – 6 pm
Fri. and Sat. . . . . 8 am – 7 pm

Whole Foods Market
2111 Briarcliff Road
Atlanta 30329
404-634-7800

Healthy fast food? Find plenty here. Largest retailer of natural and organic foods. Scratch bakeries, in-store chefs. Nice deli. Cheeses galore. Spices, grains, and organically grown produce.

Mon. – Sat. . . . . 8 am–10 pm
Sunday . . . . 8 am – 9 pm

Other Location at
5930 Roswell Road
Sandy Springs, 30328

Daily . . . . 8 am – 9 pm

Unique Places  *to Shop*

OUTLET STORES

North Georgia Premium Outlets
800 Highway 400
Dawsonville 30534
706-216-3609

It's the 25% to 65% off on name-brand fashions that makes shopping fun. Over 140 upscale stores like Nike, Liz Claiborne, Calvin Klein, Donna Karan, and more. Only 35 minutes from Atlanta. Take GA-400 N to Highway 318 (Dawson Forest Road).

Mon. – Sat. . . . . 10 am – 9 pm
Sun. . . . . Noon – 6 pm

Tanger Outlet Center
111 Tanger Drive
Commerce 30529
800-405-9555

Shop at this giant Tanger Outlet Center complex. (Actually two centers.) Over 112 stores with popular name brands such as Reebok, Disney, Dansk, Liz Claiborne, Claiborne for Men, Elizabeth, Kitchen Collection, Polo Jean Co., and much more. You'll find yourself in shopper's heaven. Take I-85 N; exit #149.

Mon. – Sat. . . . . 9 am – 9 pm
Sun. . . . . Noon – 6 pm

Unique Places to Shop

UNIQUE PLACES TO SHOP

Lenox Square & Phipps Plaza
3393 Peachtree Road N.E.
Atlanta 30326, 404-233-6767

Too much of a good thing? Not at Lenox Square, Atlanta's biggest mall. Shop Macy's, Neiman Marcus, Rich's, plus 230 other specialty stores. If you shop until you drop, there are great restaurants, a movie theater, and a luxury hotel. Across the street, Phipps Plaza's upscale stores make for more fun. Valet Parking.

Mon. – Sat. . . . . 10 am – 9 pm
Sunday . . . . Noon – 6 pm

Little Five Points

Atlanta's funky side, only do this during daylight. Often campared to New York's Greenwich Village, it's pop culture, hip stores, vintage clothing, Gothic-looking freaks, and good food. Stop for lunch at the Vortex–best burgers in Atlanta. Or terrific jerk chicken at Bridgetown Grill. (Be sure to step into Junkman's Daughter). Take I-85 and exit North Ave. Go left to Moreland Ave. MARTA: Chandler Park station.

Stone Mountain Village
Visitor Center, 891 Main Street
Stone Mountain 30083
770-879-4971

A village just for shoppers. Find shops with funnel cakes, antiques, fine art, quilts, collectibles, jewelry, books, and more. Find a leather handbag outlet and a Civil War Museum. Restaurants. Lodging. Closes at 4 pm during the winter. Fifteen miles east of Atlanta.

Mon. – Sat. . . . . 10 am – 6 pm
Thursdays . . . . open until 9 pm

Unique Places  *to Shop*

UNIQUE SHOPS

Brumby Chair Company
37 West Park Square
Marietta, 30060, 770-425-1875

Take home a little Southern comfort. Since 1875, the Brumby family has handcrafted the famous Brumby rocking chair. Made from the finest Appalachian Red Oak. World famous for craftsmanship, durability, and elegance. Five rockers sat on the White House's Truman Balcony during President Carter's administration.

Mon. – Sat. . . . . 10 am – 5 pm

Build-A-Bear Workshop
Mall of Georgia
333 Buford Highway Suite 2017
Atlanta 30519, 770-945-2990

Make a new friend to take home! One of Atlanta's most unique shops. Literally build your own teddy bear. Custom make a cow, frog, cat, dog … lots of fun. From $10 to $25.

Mon. – Sat. . . . . 10 am – 9 pm
Sunday . . . . Noon – 6 pm

Junkman's Daughter
464 Moreland Avenue N.E
Atlanta 30307
404-577-3188

Funky, hipster clothing. Pop culture. Find cool vintage clothing, new fashions, and a bit of junk. Plan to spend time browsing awhile. Shoe loft upstairs. Merchandise moderately priced.

Mon. – Fri. . . . . 10 am – 7 pm
Sunday . . . . Noon – 7 pm

January
1. Martin Luther King, Jr. Week

February
2. Southeastern Flower Show

April
3. Atlanta Dogwood Festival
4. Georgia Renaissance Festival (April - May)
5. Inman Park Spring festival

May
6. Atlanta Jazz Festival
7. Midtown Music Festival

June-October
8. Georgia Shakespeare Festival

July
9. Peachtree Road Race

August
10. Folk Fest

December
11. Egleston Children's Christmas Parade

Chapter 9
ANNUAL EVENTS

January
- Martin Luther King, Jr. Week 172

February
- Southeastern Flower Show 173

April
- Atlanta Dogwood Festival 174
- Georgia Renaissance Festival (April - May) ... 175
- Inman Park Spring Festival 176

May
- Atlanta Jazz Festival 177
- Midtown Music Festival 178

June-October
- Georgia Shakespeare Festival 179

July
- Peachtree Road Race 180

August
- Folk Fest 181

December
- Egleston Children's Christmas Parade 182

Watch For These Annual Events

MARTIN LUTHER KING, JR. WEEK

Martin Luther King, Jr. Center
449 Auburn Avenue N.E.
404-526-8900
www.kingcenter.org

(January)

A national event begins in Atlanta

Big happenings take place in Atlanta the 2nd week of January—before the Martin Luther King, Jr. National Holiday (January 15).

A commemorative church service at the historic Ebenezer Church kicks the week into action. Public welcome. Broadcast on television.

You'll find events taking place throughout the city. Tributes to the Civil Rights leader include special plays, musicals, awards dinners, seminars, films, and a parade down Peachtree Street to Auburn Avenue.

Hear speakers like Coretta Scott King. Listen to the Atlanta Symphony Orchestra perform a major concert in King behalf. The concerts broadcasted on National Public Radio. Call the King Center for more information.

Directions

Events throughout Atlanta. The King Center: From I-75/85, exit Freedom Pkwy./Center Center. Turn right on Boulevard. Follow signs. MARTA: King Memorial station.

Watch For These Annual Events

SOUTHEASTERN FLOWER SHOW

Atlanta Exposition Center
3650 Jonesboro Road S.E.
Atlanta, 30354
404-888-5638
www.flowershow.org

(Mid-February)
Atlanta blooms at this event

Before spring fever hits, discover new ideas for your backyard at the Southeastern Flower Show. A 5-day annual family event that's one of the largest of its kind.

Three acres become a celebration with new landscaping techniques and the latest in floral arranging. Find an array of waterfalls, fountains, and other landscaping items on display. Listen to seminars; watch demonstrations. Inspiring.

Benefits the Atlanta Botanical Garden.

Hours
5-day show

Wed. & Thurs	9:30 am – 6:30 pm
Fri. & Sat.	9:30 am – 8:30 pm
Sunday	9:30 am – 6 pm

Cost

Adults	$15
Children 4 - 15	$5
Two-day passes	$20
Advanced tickets	$11

Directions
East of Hartsfield International Airport.
From I-285, exit #55.

Watch For These Annual Events

ATLANTA DOGWOOD FESTIVAL

Piedmont Park
404-329-0501
www.dogwood.org

(April)

Oh, what fun it is at Piedmont Park

Who wouldn't want to be at Piedmont Park for the Dogwood Festival? It's simply 3 days of great fun. Considered the South's biggest spring-time celebration.

Bring the whole family and enjoy live entertainment, fine arts and crafts displays, a canine frisbee competition, the Kid's Village, a rock climbing wall, and hot air balloons. Eat lots of tasty food.

See incredible dog stunts, the Eco-Village, and other fun things like an electric car show. Tour elegant homes in Midtown.

Sponsored by the city of Atlanta Celebrates the city's beauty. An annual event for over 65 years. Over 200,000 people attend.

Hours

Friday	Noon – 8 pm
Saturday	Noon – 9 pm
Sunday	Noon – 7 pm

Cost

Free admission

Directions

At Piedmont Park. Piedmont Avenue and 10th Street. MARTA: Midtown station.

Watch For These **Annual Events**

GEORGIA RENAISSANCE FESTIVAL

770-964-8575
www.garenfest.com

(April - May)

Visit another time and place without leaving Georgia

Forget where you are. Eat, wander, and enjoy the atmosphere of England centuries ago—in the piney woods of Georgia.

See entertaining shows and booths. Explore the village. Great food. Dress in medieval attire, if you like. Best place for people watching.

Held on 7 consecutive weekends, ending on Memorial Day Weekend.

Plan to spend the entire day. Wear comfortable shoes. Great to go with spouse or friends. Purchase discount tickets online. Parking free.

Hours

Sat. and Sun. . . . . 10:30 am – 6 pm

Cost

Adults $14.95
Children 6 – 12 . . . . $5.95

Directions

Held in Fairburn, 8 miles south of the Hartsfield Airport on I-85. Exit #61.

Watch For These Annual Events

INMAN PARK SPRING FESTIVAL

Inman Park
770-242-4895
www.inmanpark.org

(April)

See the beautiful old homes in Inman Park

Springtime. And historic Inman Park shows off its classy old Victorian homes—a 3-day celebration. These charming homes aren't otherwise open to the public.

Claims the biggest "street market" with something for everyone. Handicrafts, dance festivals, live music, antique market, art exhibits, and more. Plenty of good food. Features a fun, quirky parade.

Held the last weekend in April. Make this one of your family's affairs.

Hours

Friday .... Noon – 4 pm
Sat. & Sun. .... Noon – 6 pm

Cost

Admission to all festival events is free.
Tour of Homes tickets are available in advance for $12, and for $15 at the Festival.

Directions

Located 2 miles of east of downtown Atlanta.

Watch For These Annual Events

ATLANTA JAZZ FESTIVAL

404-817-6851 Hot Line
404-817-6815
www.bcaatlanta.org

(May)
Atlanta rocks

Atlanta celebrates jazz.

A ten-day festival with the popular "Free Weekend Concert Series" on Memorial Day Weekend in Piedmont Park.

Considered the largest free jazz festival. Hear the best of jazz. Many a big-name star performs before other big names in the audience. Over 100 of the world's best musicians come for the festival.

Concerts are also performed at different music venues throughout the city. Admission charged.

The festival is sponsored by the city of Atlanta.

Hours
Sat., Sun., & Mon. . . . . 2 pm – 10 pm

Cost
Free Memorial Day Weekend concerts

Directions
At Piedmont Park. Piedmont Avenue and 12th Street. MARTA: Midtown station.

Watch For These Annual Events

MIDTOWN MUSIC FESTIVAL

Atlanta Civic Center
Piedmont Aveue
404-249-6400, www.musicmidtown.com

(May)

Atlanta's big music fest

Midtown rocks for 3 days in May (usually the 1st weekend). And you need to be there. One of Atlanta's best festivals.

Take in the festivities that involve nine different performing stages and over 100 musicians.

You'll find the artists' market, Kid's Town, live demonstrations, lots of good food, and more. Some of Atlanta's finest restaurants bring in food.

Purchase tickets by phone, 404-249-6400, or through Ticketmaster, 404-817-8700 (sfx.com).

Parking limited. MARTA makes a great alternative. Festival entrances near the North Avenue and Civic Center stations.

Hours

Friday	6 pm – Midnight
Saturday	Noon – Midnight
Sunday	Noon – Midnight

Cost

One-day pass	$25
Three-day pass	$30

Directions

The festival borders Ralph McGill to Pine St. and Piedmont Rd. to Bedford Pl. and includes Renaissance Park and Bedford Pines Park.

Watch For These **Annual Events**

GEORGIA SHAKESPEARE FESTIVAL

Oglethorpe University Campus
4481 Peachtree Road, 404-264-0020

(Mid-June to October)

If you like to have fun, you'll love the Shakespeare Festival. But get your tickets well in advance. Tickets go on sale as early as April.

With your ticket comes a menu. Order what you'd like for the pre-performance picnic. (Only for the summer performances.) Or bring your own picnic lunch. Picnicking takes place up to 1 1/2 hours before the show starts.

See the play in the fantastic Conant Center. The theater is adaptable to open-air as well as air-conditioned shows, depending on the weather.

Four to five productions a season. Performs classical and innovative Shakespeare and other classics.

Hours

Shows start at 8 pm

Cost

$20 – $28

Directions

From 85 N., take the N. Druid Hills exit. Go north on N. Druid Hills (stay to the left on exit ramp). Once you cross Buford Hwy. stay on N. Druid HIlls (to the right of fork in road). As road dead ends, turn right on Peachtree Rd. The university is 1.5 miles ahead. Turn at the main gate and go straight to the Arts Center at the end of the drive.

Watch For These Annual Events

PEACHTREE ROAD RACE

Atlanta Track Club
3097 E. Shadowlawn
Atlanta 30305
404-231-9064
www.atlantatrackclub.org

(July)

Atlanta's biggy 10K run

Every runners' goal–a Peachtree Road Race t-shirt.

One hundred and ten runners ran the 1st Peachtree Road Race in 1970. The 10K run is the world's largest and most famous. Now 50,000 runners participate.

It takes over 40 minutes for all the runners to cross the starting line. The racers line up for 1/2 mile at Lenox Square, where the race begins.

Racers run 6.2 miles along Peachtree Road, Atlanta's main thoroughfare.

If you're not a runner, be one of the spectators. Over 500,000 people come to watch the race.

Hours

Begins July 4 .... 7:30 am

Cost

Free for spectators

Directions

The race begins at Lenox Square in Buckhead, travels down Peachtree Road, and ends on 10th St. at Charles Allen Drive, next to Piedmont Park.

Watch For These **Annual Events**

FOLK FEST

North Atlanta Trade Center
770-932-1000

(August)
Folk Art's Hot Stuff

It's here. Find your one-of-a-kind art treasures. Self-taught artists have a heyday. See what's become the largest festival of its kind.

Held the 3rd weekend in August, at the North American Trade Center.

Works include all kinds of media: paintings, pottery, quilts, wood carvings, you name it.

On Friday, meet the artists.

Hours

Friday	5 pm – 10 pm
Saturday	10 am – 7 pm
Sunday	10 am – 5 pm

Cost

Friday	$15
Saturday	$6
Sunday	$6

Directions

In Gwinnett County, located 20 minutes from Atlanta on I-85 N. Exit #101, Indian Trail Road.

Watch For These Annual Events

EGLESTON CHILDREN'S CHRISTMAS PARADE
404-264-9348

(December)

How Santa comes to Atlanta

A big to-do in Atlanta. Santa comes. But he does it in style—lavish floats, marching bands, lots of balloons.

Atlanta's annual Christmas parade begins at 10:30 am. Starting at Marietta Street and International Boulevard, it travels down Peachtree Street to West Peachtree Street.

The parade kicks off the holiday season beginning with the Festival of Trees. See what local talent does with 200 Christmas trees surrounding the Georgia World Congress Center. Not only are there fancy decorated trees, but the festival includes arts, crafts, food, an antique carousel, and a miniature train for the kids. Free admission.

Hours
Parade
1st Saturday in December .... 10:30 am

Cost
Free

Directions
Downtown Atlanta.

Index

Symbols

1848 House 128

A

A Flea An'tique 165
Actor's Express 103
Actor's Express Theater 92
African-American Art Resource Center 100
African-American Museum 88
Agatha's A Taste of Mystery 93
Alliance Theater Company 94
Alonzo F. Herndo Home 73
American Adventures Amusement Park 108
Amicalola Falls State Park 44, 46
Anna Ruby Falls 45
Ansley Inn 154
Antique Shops 162
Apex Museum 72
Appalachian National Scenic Trail 46
Appalachian Outfitters 59
Appalachian Trail 55
Apple House 63
Arkenstone Paintball Games 118
Art Galleries 163, 164
Arts Center 99, 103
Atlanta Ballet Centre 95
Atlanta Beach at Clayton County International Park 109
Atlanta Botanical Garden 26
Atlanta Broadway Series 96
Atlanta Civic Center 178
Atlanta Convention and Visitors Center 20
Atlanta Cyclorama 11
Atlanta Dogwood Festival 30, 174
Atlanta History Center 16, 20
Atlanta Jazz Festival 30, 177
Atlanta Motor Speedway Tour 110
Atlanta Opera 97
Atlanta Preservation Center 30, 32, 112
Atlanta Rocks 111
Atlanta Skydiving Center 122
Atlanta Symphony Orchestra 98
Atlanta Track Club 180
Atlanta Walking Tours 112
AtlanTIX 20

B

Babyland General Hospital 113
Ballet, Atlanta 95
Battle of Atlanta 11, 16
Berry Patch Farms 63
Berry's Christmas Tree Farm 52
Bethany Tree Farms 52
Beverly Hills Inn 154
Birth Home Tour 22
Blood Mountain 68
Blue Ridge Mountains 68
Blue Ridge Railroad 47

Index

Blueberry Farm 63
Bones 129
Brasserie Le Coze 130
Brasstown Bald 48, 65
Braves Museum and Hall of Fame 17
Broad River Outpost 59
Broadway Series, Atlanta 96
Brumby Chair Company 169
Buckhead Diner 131
Buford Highway Flea Market 165
Build-A-Bear Workshop 169
Bull Mountain Bike Trail 61
Bulloch Hall 74
Burt's Pumpkin Farm 49
Butterfly Center 50
By Hand South 164

C

Cabbage Patch Doll 113
Callanwolde Fine Arts Center 99
Callaway Gardens 50, 160
Canoe 132
Capitol Building 40
Carrot Club 121
Carter Presidential Center & Library 75
Casual Concerts 98
Centennial Olympic Park 31
Center for Puppetry Arts 20, 76
Chamblee's Antique Row 162
Chateau ElanWinery & Resort 161
Chattahoochee and Oconee National Forest 65
Chattahoochee Nature Center 51
Chattahoochee Outdoor Center 29
Chattahoochee River National Recreation Area 29
Children's Healthcare of Atlanta Children's Garden 26
Christmas Parade 182
Christmas Tree Farms 52
Civil War Tours 114
Clayton County International Park 109
Cloudland Canyon State Park 53
CNN Center and Studio Tour 15
Coca-Cola Atlanta 34
Conant Center 179
Conncord Covered Bridge 54
Connell Gallery 163
Consolidated Gold Mines 62
Covered Bridge Trail of Georgia 54
Crisson Gold Mine 62
Cyclorama 11

D

Dahlonega Gold Museum state Historic site 77
Decatur Arts Building 104
December Farms 52
DeSoto Falls Trail 55
Discovery Center 50

Index

Doc Chey's Noodle House 133
Dockery Lake Trail 55
Dogwood Festival 174
Dukes Creek Falls 65

E

Egleston Children's Christmas Parade 182
Ellijay Apple Country 56
Emory University 25
Episcopal Cathedral of St. Philip 18
Etowah Indian Mounds State Historic Site 78
Euharlee Covered Bridge 54

F

Family Classic Theater 95
Family Concerts 98
Federal Reserve Bank of Atlanta's Monetary Museum 79
Fernbank Museum Of Natural History 19
Fernbank Science Center 80
Festival of Trees 182
Fine Arts Center 99
Flea Markets 165
Flying Biscuit Cafe 145
Foam Factory 108
Folk Fest 181
Food Markets 166
Food Studio 103
Four Season Hotel 152
Fox Theatre 18, 36
Frabel Studio and Gallery 163
Free Weekend Concert Series 177
Futral Farms Peach Orchard 63

G

Gaslight Inn 155
Georgia Dome 37
Georgia Governor's Mansion 33
Georgia Highway 197 65
Georgia Music Hall of Fame 81
Georgia Racing Hall of Fame 123
Georgia Renaissance Festival 175
Georgia Shakespeare Festival 179
Georgia Soaring Association 120
Georgia World Congress Center 182
Georgian Terrace 160
Georgis Apple Festival 56
Go With The Flow 59
Gold City Corral 58
Gold'N Gem Grubbin 62
Gooch Gap to Woody Gap 55
Grand Hyatt Atlanta 152

H

Hammonds House Galleries & Resource Center of Africa 100
Hanwoori 134
Haralson Mills Covered Bridge 54

Index

Heartfield Manor 155
Hess Tree Farm 52
High Museum of Art 18, 21, 101
Hillcrest Orchards (Apple House) 63
Historic Days Inn 158
Holiday Concerts 98
Holiday Inn Midtown North 158
Homestead Christmas Tree Farm 52
Horseradish Grill 135
Hot Air Ballooning 115

I

Ice Forum 116
Ice Skating Rinks 116
Inman Park 176
Inman Park Spring Festival 176

J

Jack's Tree Farms 52
Jackson Fine Art 163
Jake Mountain Bike Trail 61
Jazz Festival 177
Jewish Heritage Museum 89
Johnson Ferry and Power Island Outlet 29
Jomandi Productions 102
Junkman's Daughter 169

K

Kamogawa 136
Kennesaw National Battlefield Park 82
Keown Falls Scenic Area 65
King Plow Arts Center 103
King-Keith House 156
Krispy Kreme Donuts 35

L

L&N Train Depot 47
La Prada's Restaurant 65
Lake Lanier Islands Resort 60
Lake Lanier Resort 161
Lake Winfield Scott To Blood Mountain Trail 55
Lakewood Antiques Market 162
Lanier Terrace Restaurant 26
Laser Quest 119
Lawrenceville Adventures Aloft 115
Len Foote Hike Inn 44
Lenox Square 18
Lenox Square & Phipps Plaza 168
Little Five Points 12, 168
Little White House State Park Historic Site 83
Lowe Gallery 163

Index

M

Magical Night Lights 60
Malibu Speedzone 117
Mall of Georgia 169
Margaret Mitchell's House 18, 24
Marietta Atlanta Aerosports 115
MARTA 13
Martin Luther King, Jr. National
  Historic Site 22
Martin Luther King, Jr. Week 172
Mary Mac's Tea Room 137
Masterworks 98
McCaysville 47
Metropolitan Atlanta Rapid Transit
  Authority 13
Michael C. Carlos Museum 25
Mid-Georgia Soaring Association
  120
Midtown Music Festival 178
Miss Freedom 40
Moccasin Creek State Park 65
Monroe-Walton County Airport
  120
Mountain Adventures Cyclery 61
Mountain Biking 61
Mountain Music Festival 68
Mt. Katahdin 46
Mumbo Jumbo 138
Music Factory 81

N

Nava 139
Neighborhood Playhouse 104
North Atlanta Trade Center 181
North Georgia Premium Outlets
  167

O

Oakland Cemetery 41
Oglethorpe Univerisity 179
Oh . . . Maria! 140
OK Cafe 141
Old McDonald's Farm 64
Open Air Orchards 63
Opera, Atlanta 97
Organ Society 99
Outlet Stores 167

P

Paintball Atlanta 118
Paintball Playing Fields 118
Papermaking Museum 85
Parkaire Ice Arena 116
Peach Blossom Trail 65
Peachtree Road Race 180
Peachtree Street 18
Phipps Plaza 168
Piedmont Park 30, 174, 177
Pine Mountain Wild Animal Park
  64
Power Island 29
Puppetry Arts Center 76

Index

Q

QZar Games 119

R

Railway museum 87
Raven Cliffs Trail 55
Resource Center of African-American Art 100
Rhodes Hall 84
Richard Russell Scenic Highway 65
Ridge Valley Scenic Byway 65
Ridgeway Christmas Tree Farm 52
Ritz-Carlton Atlanta 153
Ritz-Carlton Buckhead 153
River Right Outfitters 59
Robert C. Williams American Museum of Papermaking 85

S

SailPlane Rides 120
Scenic Georgia Highway 197 65
SciTrek 86
Shakespeare Festival 179
Shellmont Bed & Breakfast 157
Signature Shop and Gallery 164
Six Flags Over Georgia 121
Skydive Monroe 122
Skydiving 122
Sleep Inn/Mainstay Suites 159
Snellville Balloon Safaries 115
Southeastern Expeditions 59
Southeastern Flower Show 173
Southeastern Railway Museum 87
Southern Terminus 46
Springer Mountain 46
State Capitol Building 40
Steven Stoli Playhouse and The Backyard Theater 102
Stone Mountain 23
Stone Mountain Park Covered Bridge 54
Stone Mountain Village 168
Sugar Magnolia Bed & Breakfast 156
Summerfield Suties 159
Sunburst Stables 58
Sunny Farms North 58
Super Pops 98
Swan Coach House 16, 143
Swan House 16, 28
Sweet Auburn Curb Market 166
Swissotel Atlanta 153
Symphony Orchestra, Atlanta 98

T

Tallulah Gorge State Park 66
Tanger Outlet Center 167
Taqueria del Sol 144
The Blueberry Farm 63
The Children's Healthcare of Atlanta Children's Garden 26

Index

The Country Store 49
The Ebenezer Church 22
The Flying Biscuit Cafe 145
The Lowe Gallery 163
The Organ Society 99
The Varsity 14
Theater of the Stars 105
Thelma's Kitchen 146
Thomas Orchards & Greehouse 63
Three Forks Trail 55
Thunder Road USA 123
Trackrock Stables 58
Trail Dust Steak House 142
Tray Mountain 45
Trinity Gallery Buckhead 163
Tubman African-American Museum 88
Turner Creek Bike Trail 61
Turner Field 17

U

Uncle Remus Stories 38
Underground Atlanta 20, 32
Unicoi Outfitters 57
Unicoi State Park and Lodge 67
Unique Places To Shop 168
Unique Shops 169
Upper Hi Fly 57

V

Van Gogh 164
Varsity 14
Vermilion Gallery 164
Virgina Highland Inn 157
Virtual Village 86
Vogel State Park 68
Vortex Restaurant 12

W

Watershed 147
Westin Peachtree Plaza Hotel 39
White Water Atlanta 124
Whole Foods Market 166
Wildlife Game Ranch 69
Wildwood Outfitters 59
William Breman Jewish Heritage Museum 89
Woodruff Arts Center 94
World of Music 81
Wren's Nest 38
www.actorsexpress.com 92
www.agathas.com 93
www.alliancetheater.org 94
www.animalsafari.com 64
www.apexmuseum.org 72
www.atlantaballet.com 95
www.atlantabotanicalgarden.org 26
www.atlantabraves.com 17
www.atlantamotorspeedway.com 110
www.atlantaopera.org 97
www.atlantasymphony.com 98
www.atlantatheatres.com 20
www.atlantatrackclub.org 180
www.atlhist.org 16